Advance praise for
Results from the Heart

"Suzaki reminds us to wake up to our true selves and find joy in our work. By listening to our hearts, we have the ability to paint our lives as an unfolding canvas. The 'mini-company' is the brush with which we can merge our brains with our hearts. *Results from the Heart* is a genius stroke!"

—Rob Kramer, Chairman, Uprizer, Inc.

"Is it possible to transform cogs into kings? Kiyoshi Suzaki thinks so, and here is his manual, a finely detailed and comprehensively written Tao of Work. Although the text remains concrete and practical, it also embodies the Zen action of transforming any place into a sanctuary in which we realize our individual and collective destiny. If I were to return to company life—trade in my Buddhist robes for a suit and tie—*Results from the Heart* would be my corporate bible."

—Martin Hughes, Chief Priest, Daigo-ji Zen Temple (Japan)

"In response to customer's requirements for faster, better, and cheaper, the 'mini-company' is the best tool to implement positive change into any organization. Effectively balancing the intricacies of mini-companies is best done as Suzaki points out, using a mix of heart, head, and self-management. *Results from the Heart* is a must-read for anyone embarking on the team process of continuous improvement."

—Mark Lindquist, President, Rapid-line

"*Results from the Heart* brings rigor to modern management theory, presenting its essence in a clear and approachable style. Suzaki confronts anonymity and lack of self-accountability and injects new life into taking ownership at every level of a corporation. There is much to be gleaned from his provocative thesis."

—Russ Hall, Managing Partner, Legacy Venture

"'Mini-company' must be a state of mind. It's not a specific corporate structure but a spirit that can be utilized with any organization. The spirit is one that leads to personal fulfillment for the individual and results for the company, through individuals taking responsibility and assuming initiative."

—John Shook, Partner, Lean Enterprise Institute, and author of *Learning to See*

"Since the early visits of Kiyoshi Suzaki and after ten years of practicing 'the mini-company approach,' we are becoming more and more aware that human sensitivity is the cornerstone of this new way of thinking. Thus, we are reaching a much closer link between what we think, what we feel, and what we do. This coherence and consistency is helping us to grow as individuals and as an organization."

—Pedro L. Urreta, Production Manager, Industrias del Ubierna S.A. (Spain)

"Our company has been practicing the mini-company concept for nine years. *Results from the Heart* reinforces our actions and will help motivate our associates, officers, and bankers to continuously improve on the mini-company concept. Its many well-reasoned examples provide a compelling justification for implementing such a valuable tool."

—Jim Zawacki, President, GR Spring & Stamping,
and author of *It's Not Magic*

"What allows a startup to become a truly great company is the ability to capture the human potential of the entire organization. Suzaki's model of a mini-company is a fabulous way to maintain this incredible potential throughout rapid growth. He describes building an emotional bond with your employees as the foundation for helping them find meaning in their work. This will take them from having a job to having a mission. And a mission has no boundaries."

—Mike Levinthal, General Partner, Mayfield Fund

"Applying the mini-company concept as it is described in this valuable book in many industrial and service organizations, our clients report not only the visible and permanent results in operational performance, but also—and more remarkably—the radical change in attitudes and behavior from the president to operators. Kiyoshi Suzaki is a master in creating living organizations. The mini-company concept is his artwork, and it offers the framework to enable hidden energy to flourish, rooted in a new managerial paradigm of people, their potential, and their aspirations."

—Bekaert Consulting Team, Bekaert Consulting S.A. (Spain)

"*Results from the Heart* has provided a comprehensive approach for managing our entire organization. We have found that 'mini-company' and 'glass wall management' open a whole new world to improve quality, cost, delivery, safety, and morale."

—Mark Evasic, President, Master Automatic, Inc.

"Many people want to become more creative and more innovative. Why? Because more challenges and threats face us in the global era. The mini-company is an effective way to develop a creative and innovative organization."

—Al Purwanto, General Manager,
PT.Hartono Istana Teknologi (Indonesia)

Other books by Kiyoshi Suzaki

*The New Shop Floor Management: Empowering
People for Continuous Improvement*
Kiyoshi Suzaki

*The New Manufacturing Challenge: Techniques
for Continuous Improvement*
Kiyoshi Suzaki

Just-in-Time Revolution
Kiyoshi Suzaki

*Produire Just a Temps: Les Sources de la Produc-
tivite Industrielle Japonaise*
Kiyoshi Suzaki and J. Bounine

Results

FROM THE

Heart

❖

How Mini-Company Management
Captures Everyone's Talents and Helps Them
Find Meaning and Purpose at Work

Kiyoshi Suzaki

Foreword by His Holiness
the Dalai Lama

The Free Press
New York   London   Toronto   Sydney   Singapore

fP

THE FREE PRESS
A Division of Simon & Schuster, Inc.
1230 Avenue of the Americas
New York, NY 10020

For information about special discounts for bulk purchases,
please contact Simon & Schuster Special Sales:
1-800-456-6798 or business@simonandschuster.com

Designed by Jan Pisciotta

Manufactured in the United States of America

1 3 5 7 9 10 8 6 4 2

Library of Congress Cataloging-in-Publication Data
Suzaki, Kiyoshi.
Results from the heart : how mini-company management
captures everyone's talents and helps them find meaning
and purpose at work / Kiyoshi Suzaki.
p. cm.
Includes index.
(alk. paper)
1. Small business—Management. 2. New business enterprises—Management.
3. Small business—Management—Employee participation. 4. Small business—
Employees—Psychology. 5. Employee motivation. 6. Customer relations.
I. Title: Meaning and purpose at work. II. Title.
HD62.7 .S987 2002
658.02'2—dc21   2001051113
ISBN 0–7432–1550–8

For those who never lose hope and who bring hope to the hopeless

Contents

✦

Foreword

by

His Holiness the Dalai Lama

❖

As human beings, the one factor that differentiates us from other species is our intelligence, which both expresses itself and trains itself through education. However, the development of the brain, the intellectual side of our nature, and the development of a good heart, a warm heart, must complement each other in a more balanced way. This is why, wherever I go, I always try to promote human values, the good qualities of the human mind, the good qualities of human beings. They are the source of happiness, and happiness is ultimately what each of us wants.

I believe we have both the ability and the means to solve our problems and improve our world. Perhaps the most important factors that inhibit us are short-sightedness, narrow-mindedness, and selfishness. Yet to look after yourself is not wrong. Without a strong sense of self we cannot develop self-confidence, determination, and will power. But we must be careful, for there is also a narrow-minded selfishness that can lead to self-destruction. To counter that we have to realize that in reality our own interest is closely linked to the interests of others and the benefit, happiness, and interests of others are our own.

In modern times it has become rarer for people to come up with new and original initiatives and ideas because the problems we face are so dauntingly complex. However, I understand that Kiyoshi Suzaki has developed strategies to improve people's participation in business and production from the point of view not only of the company, but also of the individual. I agree with him that if we all learned to use the brain, but at the same time to listen to the heart, we could make our world a happier, more peaceful, and successful place.

Dharamsala, India
October 4, 2001

Preface

❖

We search constantly for people, things, ideas, or experiences that ultimately touch our hearts and bring meaning to our lives. Work is where we spend a large portion of our time. Although many of us see work solely as a way to make a living, it can also provide a way to express ourselves and fulfill our potential. In this book you will read about a new business idea—the "mini-company"—that can connect your work with your personal life and enable you to become the master of your own destiny, regardless of the size of your company, the complexity of your job, or your past experiences or talent.

It is our nature to seek opportunities and strive to overcome problems. We do the best we can to enrich our lives. Whether we are president of the company or an employee, when we find a solution to a problem, we feel wonderful, and sometimes even inspired. We feel joy, and even confidence. We also sense that our lives are flowing as they are meant to. When no solution presents itself, we often feel extreme discomfort. Going back and forth in this way, we keep searching for ways to realize our potential.

At the heart of it all is our *hope* and *will* for a better life. These words may sound soft in today's hard-nosed business environment. But they are more important in today's world than ever before. If we try our best—that is, if we use our talents to the fullest—we will not fail. Our ultimate source of inspiration, i.e., revelation, will always be there to help us find our destiny even in the most difficult situations we face in business—or in life. I hope to describe how we all can connect to that source. Moreover, I hope to show how, in any company, we can capture everyone's maximum potential, thus creating a truly dynamic and lively organization that fulfills its mission.

I propose here that each of us be "promoted" to presidency of his area of responsibility, that is, his own mini-company. In essence, it is meant for the individuals and whole organization to achieve mastery in whatever we do. Not only addressing the operational issues, the strategic impact of this concept is realized when the sound management process is applied across the whole company with each mini-company addressing the needs of its customers. When this is done by collecting the potential of people with their own initiative, tremendous success will follow. It is an approach to bring out the business results by connecting the heart of each individual.

This book shows how to create and run a mini-company:

- Chapter 1 identifies the need for mini-companies and provides readers with an understanding of individual and organizational development.
- Chapter 2 describes the nature of a mini-company, the universe in which it operates, and how it can help us find our destiny.
- Chapter 3 highlights the key elements of running a mini-company.
- Chapter 4 captures the holistic picture and shows how to develop a creative environment in business.
- Chapter 5 prepares readers to start their own mini-companies, with lessons on leadership and entrepreneurship.
- Chapter 6 outlines how to start a mini-company.
- Chapter 7 shows the close link between the mini-company and corporate strategy.
- Chapter 8 makes the connection between the mini-company and our life's journey.

Results

FROM THE

Heart

❖

Chapter 1

Introduction

❖

Stock markets go up and down. New technologies, competitors, products, and services emerge suddenly. The Internet has opened up previously closed boundaries, impacting the way we do business. We see more and more people facing this turbulent environment in which opportunities as well as problems abound. In such a world, where can we find our foundation?

Instead of losing sight of our intrinsic values, we must find meaning in this seeming chaos. We must go beyond just doing our work routinely. We need a fresh and lively new paradigm to continuously find purpose in what we do. Accordingly, here are two key questions for us to answer:

- How shall we find our destiny in the turbulence?
- How should we conduct our journey?

In essence, this is about *mastery* in a turbulent business environment. It is about achieving our destiny, freedom, and self-sufficiency regardless of the situation in which we find ourselves. This will take a determined effort. It is not something that we can achieve by simply introducing a few techniques here and there. We need to develop a clear understanding of *what we do and why.*

❖ ❖ ❖

Passages

First, we need to understand what is going on around us. For example, by studying strategies companies have adopted, we can see how they have tried to find their own destiny. Business strategy is about utilizing our resources wisely and deploying ideas throughout our organization. Many people's lives are affected in this process. As we try to enrich our own lives, we need to keep in mind that this personal search will influence our business strategy. Understanding this dynamic is essential if we are to chart a course for our life's journey.

Recent strategic initiatives companies have taken include mergers and acquisitions, reengineering, downsizing, empowerment, and continuous improvement. Total Quality Management and Just-In-Time concepts have been applied in streamlining business processes. Developing a well-integrated network of suppliers and customers and breaking down business boundaries are among the ways business organizations are striving to create the highest value-added services at the lowest cost and in the shortest time possible. In our free enterprise system, new business models and technologies are constantly being developed and implemented.

Ultimately, the aim of such initiatives is to eliminate waste and create value for customers, all while outperforming the competition. The flip side of waste elimination, however, is enrichment of our work life. In other words, from a business as well as a humanistic point of view, the worst kind of waste is the waste of underutilizing our talents. While actively involved in this process, we should also be able to enjoy the fruits of our efforts as customers. In this way we can all contribute to the progress of civilization. Such is the game we all play.

The premise here is that the more we understand such business principles and the better business environment we create, the more business opportunities will arise. As a result, we can utilize people's talent to a greater extent. The opening of previously closed economies, symbolized by the breakdown of the Berlin Wall, and the wide use of the Internet have helped to fuel this change process. Such progress will drive us to continue to expand our own thinking as we tap into a growing talent pool.

The global-scale movement of people, products, services, technology, information, and capital continuously provides unknown potential yet to be harnessed. While this evolving environment presents ever greater opportunities, mistakes in handling these opportunities are exposed much more quickly than ever before. Accordingly, these dynamic changes place a constant challenge on *business and on people* to prove the reasons for their existence.

A Point of Reflection

At a top management conference sponsored by a major global company, a senior executive summarized his views on current business conditions:

- The playing field is too complex to oversee all relevant details from a central viewpoint.
- The playing field is evolving very rapidly.
- Trends in technology and markets are detected at the operational level in the organization.

His conclusions were as follows:

- Hierarchical information flow is not effective.
- Hierarchical control is impractical or impossible.
- Hierarchical decision making is too slow.

As a result, he argued, management is not about "control" as practiced in the traditional sense, but about "making sense out of chaos." Having worked with hundreds of companies around the world as a management consultant, I would agree. "Chaos" reigns, not only in large global organizations but also in small manufacturing or service companies in virtually all industries. How then can a manager be effective in what he does? How can he or she make sense of a chaotic situation while retaining control? In large or small companies, private or public institutions, these critical questions demand answers.

The Challenge

How do we use our intelligence to make good judgments? How should we manage our own areas of responsibility? These are critical questions. If we can answer them, we have a good chance of finding our destiny—even in today's turbulent environment. If we cannot answer them, we may be lost or blown away before we know it.

Here, we may find that our outer world is a reflection of our inner world and that our minds are influenced by business practices while business reflects how our minds function. So, if we do not know who we are, or what we do and why, the outer world may dictate our choices and we may end up losing our balanced perspective—to the point of becoming slaves to the environment. Today's business environment can in fact be frightening. I have seen some managers, obsessed by ego, relentlessly pushing people. I have spoken with others who say that they cannot wait to retire and never think of their job again. If the goal of business is to make customers happy, why do some of us feel like victims and why are we unhappy at work? Is our mission lost and forgotten? Let us try to make sense out this chaos and discover something important that can be the foundation of our lives.

> *"Modern industrial society often strikes me as being like a huge self-propelled machine. Instead of humans being in charge, each individual is a tiny, insignificant component with no choice but to move when the machine moves."*
> (Dalai Lama in *Ethics for the New Millennium*)

Knowing Ourselves

Our modern world makes enormous demands on us and in some cases forces us to behave in a mechanical fashion. Without realizing it, we may be losing our connection with our core values. There are too many things to do, beginning in early childhood, and too much information to process just in the course of our daily lives. There is too little time to reflect. Without realizing that we have a choice—we *can* play an active role—we become passive and robotic. We should ask ourselves if we are spinning our wheels.

The following symptoms may indicate that we are too passive and robotic:

- We follow a prescribed program and lack initiative.
- We don't pay much attention to our surroundings.
- We follow others' expectations rather than our own beliefs.
- If we think we have a solid self, and believe we are always right without any doubt.

Instead of trying to understanding ourselves and relate to our surroundings better, we may blame the external world for our problems. The following story from more than two thousand years ago in Greece resonates even today.

In the temple at Delphi, the phrase "Gnoti sauton" (know yourself) is chiseled into the stone. Referring to this, Socrates asked one of his disciples, "Have you paid any attention to that phrase? Have you thought about who you are?"

"No, I have not," said the disciple. "Because I know about myself quite well. If I do not know, how can I know anything else?"

"If that is so," Socrates asked, "do you think a person who knows only his name is one who knows himself? A buyer of a horse does not know the horse until he sees if the horse is gentle or violent, strong or weak, or fast or slow. In such case, do you think a person who knows what kind of character he has and what he is good at is a person who knows himself?"

"I have not thought about myself that seriously."

"Then, you have to start making efforts to know yourself today. Nothing is as important as knowing yourself, because people who know themselves will find out what is beneficial for them, and can distinguish what they can or they cannot do."

Asking "So What?"

No matter what environment we find ourselves in, knowing ourselves is the foundation for living our life in harmony with our intrinsic nature. Finding the meaning in what we do is embodied in what I call the "So what?" principle. The point is to question ourselves repeatedly until we cannot go any further. Ultimately, we should find deep meaning in what we are doing to the point where we can fully identify ourselves with our actions. The series of answers we provide before getting to the core should help clarify the logic of *what we do and why.* To make this process work, however, we must keep asking questions and make a strong effort to answer them sincerely.

In other words, repeatedly asking "So what?" is to be honest with ourselves, and to clarify the reasons for our actions. Even if we do not arrive at a clear understanding immediately, this continuous questioning will eventually help us to understand the task better and orient us to do what is meaningful and right. Further, it should help us lay the foundation for becoming a fully qualified president of our own minicompany—that is, master of our own destiny.

Take an example. If we are contemplating some task at work, we may ask "So what?" or "What is the meaning of the task?" The response might be, "I do this because my boss asked me to do so." Instead of stopping there, let's ask "So what?" or, "If the boss gets a good report, then what?" Then, we may say, "It is important because he needs to present this report to the customers." We may again ask, "So what?" or "Why is it important?" The answer may be, "Because this customer is important for our business." We may further ask why that is so. Or we may ask what will happen if they are satisfied.

If we are to spend our valuable time on something, should we just do that task without attaching much *thought or initiative* to it? This is a critical question. If people wait for orders to be given, their company will not accomplish much or be lively or fun. These people will have little in common except collecting their paychecks.

Here is another example. If we have failed to meet a certain goal and our business unit is losing money, we ask, "So what?" We may respond, "I feel bad about it." Again, we ask, "So what?" This time, we are asking to be practical and not to dwell on our failure. In other words, we should ask what happened, what we have learned, and what we can do with the lessons learned. Obviously, we need to cut out unnecessary, unproductive thinking and focus our attention on what is meaningful, and do-able. Otherwise, it is like continuing to polish clay, in the belief that it will eventually turn into a mirror.

Ultimately, this series of questions should be connected to our *mission* so that clarity in logic and conviction are tied to our actions. What this means is that, if we repeatedly question, we should eventually touch the core of our being. That is when we feel in our hearts the source of the energy and the meaning of our work. On the other hand, if we cannot clearly explain what we do and why, there is a missing link between the task and how it contributes to accomplishing the mission. If our hearts are not in the right place in such a case, we cannot engage our full potential to the task. Naturally, we will find a vivid difference in productivity and the quality of our work between these two cases.

As more people practice "So what?" questioning and come up with a better understanding of the meaning of their work, they will begin to take the initiative to address issues on their own. Then, such an organization will begin to behave like all cells of a body self-activated to work with a sound underlying principle. Collectively, people will work for the success of the organization as well as for themselves. They will clarify the meaning and purpose in their existence as well as in their relationships with colleagues. This will help in collecting business intelligence, reducing redundancy, and enabling people to respond to their needs of the company.

Still, some may argue that not everybody is willing or capable of participating in this process. If that is so, should people be treated like a collection of robots? Should top management step in even though they are far away from the scene of the action? On the contrary, if people closer to the action ask these questions and make decisions, they will have more "control" and greater responsiveness to meet competitive threats. Not only that, they will create a dynamic, energized organization that may even produce miracles!

In summary:

- Asking "So what?" is to be honest—from the heart.
- Asking "So what?" brings out pragmatic and positive attitudes instead of wishful thinking.
- Asking "So what?" enables us to use our initiative to do our job rather than waiting to be told what to do.
- Asking "So what?" leads to discovery of the meaning of work and the ability to connect it to social needs.
- Asking "So what?" clarifies the logic that connects us to our mission and helps us bring out the full potential within us.

In chapters 2 and 3, questions like "So what?" are provided to assist readers in running their mini-companies. People need to develop a habit of coming up with the *right* questions, as those will set the boundaries of our thinking. Then, the ability to come up with thoughtful answers is prerequisite to running a mini-company successfully.

Listening to Our Heart

Let us next look at the picture from another angle. While asking "So what?" helps to clarify our thoughts, ultimately our hearts must be engaged as well. Here, "heart" represents our initiative, creativity, and the core of our being. Instead of "pushing our logic" from our brains, "listening to our heart" corresponds to being open to receiving inspiring messages coming from within.

Beyond finding insights on problems we face at work, being attentive to that voice in the heart will help us understand our true nature as well. When we feel vulnerable or lost—and even when we feel successful—we need a moment to be humble and to listen carefully to our hearts without reacting emotionally or impulsively. In fact, to explore our full potential, we should learn to distinguish the various noises surrounding us. We are reaching beyond conventional logic here, and this point is difficult to put into words. Yet, that is the very reason that *each of us* needs to listen to our heart.

Figuratively speaking, the process of coming up with the insight may be compared to "a game of catch" between our brains and our hearts. The "So what?" questions involve our brain, but the answers come from our heart. When we find an answer, we have conviction that life flows smoothly. As much as our business reflects what is in our mind, the process of clarifying the issues in business should be ultimately tied to this very point.

Let us take an example of such clarification and insight-generation process. Assume that you are the boss, and you must reach a mutual understanding with a subordinate about certain tasks to be performed. Asking a series of "So what" questions has established that the tasks are important and must be done. Yet, wait, do you sense a "vibration" that this subordinate is willing to do the tasks—with initiative and conviction?

Here is another example, this time about listening to our own hearts. Let's say we believe we know what we need to do. It may be about writing a report. Yet, after asking "So what?" repeatedly, something may still be bothering us. In such a state can we say we have done a good job?

Listening to the voice coming from the heart requires a quiet moment undisturbed by self-centered logic or emotion. We need to *let go* of ourselves, *observe* what is going on, and *listen* to the inner voice with an open mind. If we can do this, we are like a mother who intuitively understands the message of her baby. It is like having a good antenna that allows us to distinguish a voice, and to make sense of what it is saying. Logic by itself does not pick up such subtlety. On the contrary, the logic we thought valid may in fact represent our own narrow-minded and selfish viewpoint.

In the example of the subordinate, we want to know if his initiative is connected to his heart. In our own example, the question is whether we are convinced that the task is important. Logic alone cannot "move" or "engage" us to act. As discussed later, the subjects of leadership, entrepreneurship, and creativity are all related to this point. They are all about creating a *condition* to discover a *channel* to bring the insight or genuine initiative from our heart.

In summary:

- Listening is being open to unknown possibilities.
- Listening is connecting to the very source of our initiative in doing our job.
- Listening is finding meaning in work that we can believe in.
- Listening is letting our heart speak directly to us without any filter.
- Remember that we must create a quiet moment if we are to listen well. We cannot listen when we are talking, confused, or "pushing our logic."

Connecting Brain and Heart

Kant, an eighteenth-century German philosopher, had a similar concern as to how we use our brains and hearts. He said, "Concept without intuition is meaningless. Intuition without concept is blindness." Here, "concept" corresponds to the brain and "intuition" to the heart. Similarly, Einstein said "science without religion is meaningless. Religion without science is lame." Whether the subject is science, philosophy, or management, mastery is tied to finding the *channel* to connect brain and heart, thus eliciting an integral or balanced solution.

If we arrive at solutions this way, whatever work we do will be the expression of both brain *and* heart. And this should be the basis of running both our business and our personal lives in a harmonious manner. This is the most basic human process. Yet, don't we often ignore this point, hence causing undue conflict or waste? Are we too busy to set aside a quiet moment to ask ourselves the critical questions and listen for the answers that come from the heart?

Einstein also said "Imagination is power." In addition to being logical in business, we must ignite this power that each of us has within. Doing so will require dedication and careful coordination of our actions. Earlier, we questioned whether the key concern for managers is "control." Ultimately, each of us must find our own destiny while connecting it to the mission of our organization.

Antoine de Saint-Exupéry said, "If you want to build a ship, don't gather your people and ask them to provide wood, prepare tools, assign tasks. . . . Just call them together and raise in their minds the longing for the endless sea." In a nutshell, this expresses the point of listening to our heart and finding the source of initiative and creative energy within us. Then, we have our brain and other resources available to us that can be put into effective use. In the following chapters, we will explore ways to channel our creative energy in a manner that utilizes the resources productively. It is as if we search for a harmonious solution of our brains *and* hearts with heart being the ultimate driver.

Chapter 2

Setting Up the Mini-Company

❖

The mission is the reason for a company's existence. To accomplish its mission the company needs to generate funds. The dream has to go with reality. Even a nonprofit organization has to have donations to keep its operation going. Any living organism must obtain food to sustain life or generate energy for growth, and a company is not an exception. Initiative and growth have to go hand in hand.

Addressing such a fundamental point provides a way of introducing a brand-new business concept: the mini-company. Unlike traditional management, a mini-company will create a sense of ownership. The mini-company president and its members will be able to find their destiny and meaning at work without getting lost in the turbulence of the whole organization. The end result is an evolving organization that is fully competitive yet friendly to people.

What Is a Mini-Company?

To run a company successfully, a president should be able to perform several key managerial jobs effectively. The more successful the company is, the more confidence the investors or bankers will develop in that company. In turn, the track record will help the president and his colleagues explore further opportunities.

If we think about it, the same situation applies *within* each company as well. If we view the next process as the customer and the previous process as the supplier, then every individual in the organization can in fact be viewed as the president of his or her area of responsibility, providing services or products to satisfy customers. So, let us call each of these relationships a "mini-company." In this sense, everybody is running a mini-company. Moreover, every unit or every department is a mini-company, and each task force, committee, or project team is a mini-company as well.

In one sense, it may appear as though every unit of the organization is operating independently rather than as a team. Yet, the customer-supplier relationship among units of organization will provide a vital checks-and-balances mechanism to assure customer orientation. End users will provide feedback to show if the services of the whole company are satisfactory or not. Of course, bankers, or bosses, should guide mini-companies while promoting self-management for the people there.

In a practical sense, the mini-company is a group of people working together to accomplish a common mission at work. To contribute what they can to satisfy customers, all mini-companies have to prove their reason for existence—for adding value to the end product. Whether we call it a mini-company or not, all units and members of the organization have to work with this guiding principle.

A key point here is to look at what is controllable and what is not. If we ask "So what?" about whatever we do at work and can keep coming up with answers, we will focus on key issues that are controllable and not consume our energy on what is uncontrollable. An effective manager will leave things alone if expending effort on them does not add value, or if those things are out of his or her control. We also must resist becoming emotionally involved in issues if we know that our involvement will not bear any fruit. In this way, we can learn to listen to our heart and use our brain more effectively.

Purpose

Running a mini-company can serve a variety of purposes. For its members, the main purpose is finding meaning in their work and controlling their destiny. For bankers (bosses), the mini-company helps to allocate resources and to clarify roles and responsibilities. Bankers also help the mini-company develop a comprehensive supporting framework to accomplish its mission. The mini-company addresses key customer needs. Suppliers find that mini-companies help clarify certain tasks required to accomplish their own missions and streamline the communications process. For the organization as a whole, actively involving everyone in the company creates a dynamic and lively environment to achieve the company's overall mission.

In short, the purpose of running a mini-company is to:

- Clarify management structure, reporting systems, roles and responsibilities, and accountability throughout the company.
- Practice customer orientation by involving everyone.
- Encourage initiative.
- Allocate resources according to needs.
- Find the meaning of work and our own destiny.
- Develop a common language for doing business.
- Utilize the potential of everyone in the organization.
- Create a dynamic and lively organization by engaging everyone.

As we learn more about the mini-company concept and put the idea into practice, these benefits should become self-evident.

Organization of a Mini-Company

The mini-company brings a sense of ownership to everyone in the organization. It challenges the mini-company president to use initiative to self-manage his or her business. The key focus should be on satisfying internal or external customers by utilizing available resources. Obviously, if we cannot satisfy customers, we cannot accomplish our mission nor justify our reason for existence. For any company to function smoothly, this idea has to be internalized by all units of the company, including operations, sales and marketing, engineering, R&D, human resources, finance, and all other line and staff functions.

As shown in exhibit 2.1, each mini-company will have a set of bankers (bosses), customers, suppliers, and members (employees). The term banker may sound funny. The point is to bring a sense of ownership to the people in the mini-company while its leaders provide resources and advice. So, they behave like bankers, venture capitalists, or shareholders of the mini-company. We should note that the structure of the mini-company is the same for the president of the company, vice presidents, managers, or the front-line operators. The only difference is its scope of responsibility and the nature of the work.

Exhibit 2.1
Mini-Company's Relationship with Other Stakeholders

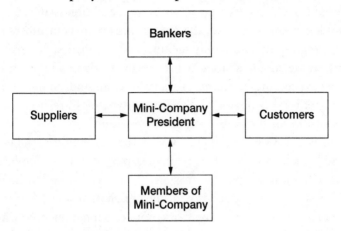

To be more specific, an example of a company is shown in exhibit 2.2 to indicate the relationships among customer, supplier, banker, and members of the mini-company.

Exhibit 2.2
Mini-Company Structure as Viewed from Different Levels
(Example)

President of Mini-Company	Customer	Supplier	Banker	Members
Operator	Operator downstream	Operator upstream	Supervisor	Machine, tools, etc.
Supervisor	Supervisor downstream	Supervisor upstream	Manager	Operators et al.
Production Manager	Shipping department	Receiving department	V.P. of Manufacturing	Supervisors et al.
V.P. of Manufacturing	Distributors, end users	Sales, engineering	President	All reporting to him
President	Users, community	Suppliers	Bankers, shareholders	All reporting to him

Even though the scope of work may vary, we can see that everyone serves as the president of a mini-company, from the front-line operator to the president. A person in a staff function is the president of his or her mini-company with its own suppliers, customers, and so on. And in addition to the stakeholders mentioned here, there are others such as members of the community and family members of employees. As appropriate, we should share our progress with them and listen to their voices and concerns. Also, gaining an understanding of competitors' behavior and industry dynamics are necessary requisites for the mini-company's operation.

It is always useful to clarify who the customers, suppliers, and bankers are, and their relative importance in accomplishing the mini-company's mission. It is also a good idea to draw a customer-supplier relationship chart from each mini-company's viewpoint. The stockroom of a medium-sized California manufacturer is shown in exhibit 2.3 as an example.

Exhibit 2.3
Customer-Supplier Relationship Chart for a Stockroom Mini-Company

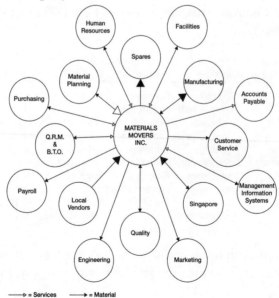

----▷ = Services ----▶ = Material

Here, thick arrows indicate strong relationships with certain customers or suppliers. Bankers or suppliers may also be seen as customers since they receive reports or suggestions. Notice also that the customer-supplier relationship is seen mostly as reciprocal, with other mini-companies indicating various material and information flows in and out of this mini-company. In this example, people came up with a name for their mini-company to promote their own identity. The name, Materials Movers Inc., appropriately illustrates the importance of moving materials in and out of the stockroom, as opposed to emphasizing the non-value-added process of simply stocking materials.

If we consolidate exhibits like this for all mini-companies, we should come up with a picture of the convoluted linkages across all levels and all functions of the organization. That integrated entity of mini-companies may be compared to the neuron network in the human brain. Exhibit 2.4 contrasts a conventional, hierarchical organization with a neuron-type organization in which mini-companies are connected with customer-supplier relationships among themselves. As compared to simply following the chain of command in a hierarchically functioning company, responding to the needs of customers is seen as the primary driving force in a mini-company. Even though hierarchical flexible command is still respected, a self-initiated approach is emphasized. In a way, this represents a web-type flexible structure with a decentralized network of computers linked by the Internet, as compared to processing information on a centralized mainframe computer.

Exhibit 2.4
Comparison of Conventional and Neuron-Type
Organizations

Conventional Organization
- Power driven
- Rigid structure
- Cumbersome to coordinate

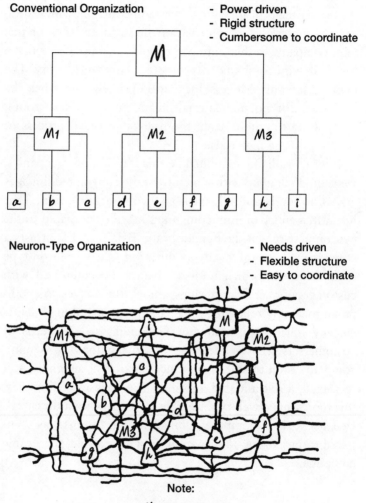

Neuron-Type Organization
- Needs driven
- Flexible structure
- Easy to coordinate

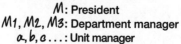

Note:
M: President
M1, M2, M3: Department manager
a, b, c . . . : Unit manager

As discussed more in detail later, no matter how complex the organization may appear, the key elements of management will be its mission, objectives, business plans, and the reporting structure. Here, the bankers are expected to review the progress of mini-companies, provide guidance, assure linkage to the overall goals of the organization and allocate resources to execute the strategy. Review meetings may be called bankers' meetings, where typically the banker (boss) sets the heartbeat so that the mini-company's operation is evaluated at regular intervals. Similarly, the mini-company president will manage the operation with the mini-company's members, utilizing everyone's talents.

From Hierarchical to Self-Initiating

The important checks and balances of a mini-company operation are also achieved by cross-functional communications based on customer-supplier relationships. Since hierarchical control often requires much time and effort, self-initiated communication among mini-companies becomes crucial to autonomous management. Then, as more mini-companies use their own initiative to help each other, the vitality and business performance of the organization will improve.

The person with an authoritative nature may find it difficult to rely on such a process. However, competition and various changes imposed on business are forcing us to always seek for better solutions. Then, because customer-supplier relationships are reciprocal, typically we find that people are generally motivated and very willing to help each other. Given opportunity and proper guidance, people often make comments like, "This time I got the help. Next time, it'll be my turn to help him." Such initiatives can lead to the development of a "self-managing organization."

Of course, traditional or top-down supervision may be necessary when the mini-company is lacking in certain capabilities or has not yet earned the confidence of its bankers. However, as a sense of ownership develops and the ability of the mini-company is proven, the shift of roles and responsibility should take place, enabling the mini-company to manage its business by itself. Developing the necessary skills for mini-company operation corresponds to strengthening the brain's network of neurons. As communication among those involved becomes closer, quicker, and more accurate, it resembles a soccer game played as a team as opposed to blindfolded players directed by remote control from somewhere outside the stadium.

As these processes become coordinated, the organization will grow on its own by demonstrating the ability to self-organize. In fact, as will be explained later, such initiatives can extend beyond company boundaries to create a truly networked business environment where most value-added linkages will be pursued following the principle of the free enterprise system. The limit is our imagination.

The Basics of a Mini-Company

Having discussed the structure and aim of mini-company operations, let us next look into its actual operating framework. The list shown below covers the basic elements of a mini-company. In short, it addresses who we are, what we do, why, and how we can progress further. The list should not be surprising as it is tied to what we do at work. Rather, it should be looked at more as common sense. Still, because the success or failure of mini-company operation is based on practicing these principles, we need to *understand* why these items are developed and how we *practice* them.

A Mini-Company:

- Has a mission.
- Makes customer satisfaction the number-one priority.
- Has specific objectives to accomplish its mission.
- Provides a scoreboard to monitor progress.
- Conducts regular meetings to discuss problems and opportunities.
- Acquires necessary skills, e.g., problem-solving skills.
- Develops plans of action to achieve the objectives.
- Executes plans.
- Reports progress to the bankers and peers, e.g., bankers' meetings, annual reports.
- Shares accomplishments, e.g., the mini-company open day.
- Practices the PDCA (plan-do-check-act) cycle.
- Practices glass wall management.

Note: To help a mini-company create a setting to share critical information, a concept called glass wall management is introduced. The basic idea is to display the information that is important so that even strangers can understand it without asking questions. All of the items listed above should be made visible on the display, i.e., the glass wall.

The items on this list will be covered in chapters 2 and 3. The idea of glass wall management is discussed in detail in chapter 4. Before moving on to the specifics, however, let us prepare ourselves so that we have a general understanding of why we want to take this journey.

Taking Initiative in Our Journey

Running down the list of Basics of a Mini-Company, it may appear that there is nothing new here. To think through this, however, let us review the case of hiring a new manager.

Here, this person is expected to:

- Understand his responsibility (mission)
- Satisfy customers (internal or external to the company)
- Accomplish the objectives of the company
- Utilize the talent of people and other resources to solve problems by coming up with ideas, and execute them
- Share the progress with the boss (bankers)

These points are almost identical to the items listed as the Basics of a Mini-Company. So why are such basics important? To answer, each of us has to review his own job carefully to see how these basics are not just understood in concept but *practiced effectively and efficiently with evidence*—especially in the following areas:

Taking initiative
Instead of being told what to do and simply following the boss's orders, the president of the mini-company is expected to take the initiative to actively manage the business involving his people. The traditional model of "Do as I say" as boss and "Just tell me what to do" as subordinate cannot work well in this rapidly changing business environment. The key is initiative to go over whatever hurdles are ahead of us to accomplish a mission we believe in—even overcoming our own negative emotions, fixed mind-set, or habits.

Seeking our own growth
To make the mini-company function, all members need to work together to enable everyone to grow and manage themselves better. Accomplishing the mission requires this. Growth also requires that bankers (bosses), suppliers, and customers participate fully. In this way, it involves the growth of every individual in the organization at large.

Struggling to accomplish the mission

Balancing business success with customer satisfaction while seeking meaning in our work becomes a continuous struggle to resolve conflicts. We cannot avoid this—we should face it directly. We are here to express our potential by solving problems and accomplishing our mission.

Fully utilizing our talents

A robot does not struggle. A robot does not have our creativity. A robot is dead while we are alive. Each of us should apply our unique talents and contribute our best efforts. Some may be good at solving problems; others at leading people or contributing other unique abilities. Let us put our talents to use, and let us express ourselves by finding and pursuing our mission.

Having fun along the way

While there is struggle in life, we can also find enjoyment. There will be times when we feel vulnerable or out of control. However, if we do our best using all we have, we should be able to say, "It is OK" no matter what the outcome is. Instead of victimizing ourselves, we should find ways to be the master of the situation while still having fun.

Finding meaning in work

Simply doing the task at hand does not mean we are managing our own destiny, or utilizing resources in a meaningful way. If we picture ourselves retired and reflecting on the years spent on the job, can we say with pride and conviction that the time was well spent? Just like "So what?" questioning, we should ask ourselves this important question repeatedly.

Demonstrating a reason for our existence

Having been given life on this earth, what can we do to contribute the most while utilizing the best of what we have?

Our whole being will be the answer to the question of the reason of our existence. It is our heart and the light in our eyes that should speak for themselves. We need to remember that many "programs" fail because companies did not seek out people's genuine initiatives and utilize their creative talents.

Key Messages
- If we cannot find the initiative within ourselves to explore our future, we are like robots.
- Whatever the situation we fall into, let us never lose hope.

Creating a Mini-Company's Mission

Let us go through the list in the Basics of a Mini-Company item by item. The first critical subject is the mission. The mission should represent the initiative of people who have established a vision. This vision should transcend minor differences of opinions. The mission statement should capture the spirit of people working together on such a challenge. It should be developed by mini-company members, not the boss. The mission is the answer to "So what?" in relation to the mini-company's business. It should be connected to the heart of each individual—that is, the source of creativity and passion.

Even though there should be a link to the overall mission of the company, ownership of the mini-company's mission should stay at the mini-company level. Bankers (bosses) can make suggestions and give advice. But in the end, the members of the mini-company should own it, with bankers' approval. However, what if the mission developed by the people is "To make money," or "To be well paid"? Should the bankers approve such a mission? Would we be proud to post such a mission on the glass wall? Here are some things that need to be a part of a mission in order for it to serve its purpose.

- The mission should be for the mini-company to add value and satisfy customers. The mission can only be accomplished when we follow the laws of nature. We need to know our strengths and weaknesses and understand our business environment to sort out what the mission should be.

- The members of the mini-company, bankers, suppliers, and customers, should all approve the mission. Since the mini-company cannot exist without the help of others, it is important to incorporate the ideas of key shareholders. If discrepancies are found, this may provide an occasion to develop a mutual understanding in coming up with the resolution.

- The mission should explain "what to do, and why." The mission is the reason why the mini-company exists. It is about what people hope to become. The statement should touch the core of the mini-company's being and invigorate its members to act as a team. It is a guiding principle that drives energy for the mini-company to function.

- The mission should guide everyone's activity. Any deviation from the mission should be seen as a problem requiring resolution. If the mission represents the intrinsic values of the members, any corrective action should be autonomous—that is, people will help each other resolve problems together.

- The mission may be modified to respond to changes in the environment or some new awareness on the part of the mini-company members. Anything living will go through changes. Some events may bring hardship while others present opportunities for growth. There may be changes in staff, customers, or suppliers. Facing new situations, and reflecting on lessons from the past, the mission statement may be updated to reflect the new insights.

Here are the key questions relating to the mission of the mini-company:

- Can you explain the mission of the mini-company?
- Why is this mission important for you?
- What are the critical points of the mission and what are the weaknesses that need work?
- Do you feel good about satisfying your customers?
- How is the mini-company mission tied to your personal mission? How about your boss's mission?

If the mission does not drive people to act, it should not be called a mission. The mission needs to be tied to the inner energy of people to serve its purpose. We do not want to be wandering about without having any meaningful aim in business—or in life.

If we believe the work we do has meaning, it does not matter what that work is—whether it is janitorial work or managing a billion-dollar corporation. Instead, if we cannot truthfully do our job with pride and initiative but feel dissatisfied, nothing good will come out. So it is critical that we find the mission with which each of us can truly identify. This may require some serious soul searching.

Key Messages
- The mission should inspire people to act.
- The mission should connect with people's inner energy.
- The members of the mini-company should be able to answer questions about the mission.

Clarifying the Customer-Supplier Relationship

The mini-company's members should develop a "customer-supplier relationship chart" to clarify the universe it operates in. This process is important because each mini-company should focus on addressing the needs of key customers and suppliers directly while eliminating unnecessary steps typical of most hierarchical organizations.

Exhibit 2.3 depicted a customer-supplier relationship chart. The arrows in the chart represent information or goods delivered from a mini-company to other mini-companies. Creating such a simple chart may also expose certain organizational problems. For example, when I visited the accounting department of a Spanish company, its customer-supplier relationship chart on the glass wall caught my attention. All the chart's arrows were pointing toward this accounting mini-company and nothing pointed outward. Immediately, questions were raised, such as "Why do you exist?" and "Why are these suppliers also not customers and receiving guidance from accounting?"

As we develop such a chart, and study the nature of information and goods handled by mini-companies, we may be surprised to realize the variety of activities that take place. Of course, problems will arise if there are missing links, slow response, waste in the process, or poor quality. Just as the brain's network of neurons exchanges information seamlessly, the key to a well-run organization is a well-connected network that provides value-added processing with customer-friendly services.

To "check and balance" our own act, here are key questions that must be asked about customers and suppliers:

- Which customers are critical and why?
- Which suppliers are critical and why?
- How do you provide adequate services?
- How do you prioritize your actions?
- How do your actions relate to accomplishing the mission?

As the accounting mini-company example showed, we should not just assume we know the answer. We need to see *evidence* of the mini-company in action—on the glass wall if what it does is important. Often, talking is like clouds that disappear from the sky, while organized information can expose problems much more quickly and facilitate collecting the wisdom of people.

Clarity is the key. Whether the mini-company is at the top or first level of management, all mini-companies should answer these questions. The key to a mini-company's success is its ability to identify the important needs of each of these customers, to establish some balance among them, and to work out plans that will satisfy them. To accentuate the key message, it is also a good practice to exhibit a sample of the service or product provided on the glass wall, while also highlighting customer concerns. Information about its competitors and other stakeholders may be posted as well. We need to be practical in running the business, and not ask for the perfect answer. Yet we have to make a conscious effort. A visual display functions as an important reminder to keep people focused on satisfying customers.

Key Messages
- Let us define the universe we live in using a customer-supplier relationship chart.
- Let us see if our actions are addressing the needs of our customers.

Customer Service

The nature of business is defined by a chain of customer-supplier relationships. The mini-company needs to identify and control the critical points of operation in order to provide good service to its customers. To do this, it is critical to understand customers' needs and to establish a good customer feedback loop. Of course, customers may be both inside and outside the company.

Here are key questions related to customer service:

- Do you provide services with customer friendliness in mind?
- Are the criteria by which customers evaluate your mini-company's service clear?
- Do you have good customer feedback mechanisms in place to assure the link between customers and your mini-company? May I see an example?
- Do you visit customers to get firsthand information and review progress with them?
- Do you care for your customers? If so, where is the evidence?

Whether a mini-company is really customer oriented or not is readily tested by having its members play the role of its customers. Is the transaction performed purely mechanically? If we claim to be customer-focused, our relationships with customers must have a human touch. If this is not the case, the foundation of the business needs to be reinvestigated from the beginning.

If we are playing the role of mini-company president, we have to understand the members' viewpoints to be able to communicate effectively with them. The process is also reciprocal. For example, if a mini-company member proposes an idea to the president, he needs to see his president as a customer. Hence, understanding the president's viewpoint is also important.

In the end, the mini-company brings to the customer its collective intelligence and efforts in the form of a product or service. If we put our hearts into conducting our jobs, I am sure that we will find no "lies" in the product or service that we deliver to customers. Otherwise, we should reevaluate the whole basis of business from scratch.

Key Messages
- Identify with customers.
- Our product or service represents our total efforts.

Setting Up Objectives and a Scoreboard

The idea here is "what gets measured gets done." As fulfilling the mission and achieving customer satisfaction are the core of running any business, we need to make sure that the objectives reflect the concerns of all stakeholders: customers, bankers, suppliers, and all members of the mini-company.

In nature, every living species has a nerve system with various parameters to monitor its health. Any sign of trouble is received as a signal to take action: when hungry, eat, or when tired, rest. It is the same with the mini-company. Key parameters are set to monitor how it is functioning to accomplish its mission. Since its own health is at stake, and people in the mini-company should know their business better than anyone else, the initiative to set objectives and manage the process should come from within. Of course, members of the mini-company should have the initiative to collect the information and organize it for their own sake.

If there are any overriding concerns for the health of the total organization, the mini-company needs to respond accordingly rather than putting its own interests first. We need to aim for total optimization—not suboptimization done at the mini-company level. However, for this to happen, a comprehensive nerve system must be developed to detect such problems or opportunities. There should be a platform—for example, a glass wall—where information is exchanged and judgments made.

There are two parts to setting the objectives. One is to select the key performance indicators; the other is to set the specific target level for each indicator. After the mini-company members consult with key stakeholders, the performance indicators and target levels will be set with the bankers giving final approval. The process is like playing a game of catch to agree upon the desired future outcome, considering such factors as opportunities, threats, risks, resource availability, timing, and people's talent.

By using the Pareto principle to focus on the vital few items instead of many trivial ones, the key objectives should become the main focus. Typically, for ease of monitoring from the bankers' point of view, common measurements can be used across various mini-companies. For example, a manufacturing operation may use quality, cost, delivery, safety, and morale. Here, quality, cost, and delivery represent customer satisfaction, whereas safety and morale may represent the satisfaction of mini-company members themselves. It should be noted that too ambitious objectives may result in dissipation of resources and the destruction of morale whereas not ambitious enough objectives may leave people unchallenged.

Key performance indicators should be monitored on a scoreboard, a form of glass wall, just like those used in sports competitions. Even a stranger should be able to tell if the mini-company is winning or losing the game. Yet, because information has value only when it brings people to a certain level of awareness and motivates them to action, we should ask, "So what?" or "What is the meaning?" and come up with ideas to bring the information to life. This is the idea behind glass wall management. Numbers without explanation may be called "Post Office Management" since the numbers are simply passed on without adding much intelligence to them.

It is important for a mini-company to set up a clear, comprehensive information system. If an information traffic jam develops, it must be cleared up by the members themselves. We need to understand how we are "playing the game": what is important, why, and what to do. Then, setting objectives and monitoring progress on the glass wall or scoreboard should bring people together to focus on key issues. Lack of clarity may be due to a lack of leadership, organizational problems, or the lack of analytical capability to sort out the issues.

Failure by the mini-company to resolve such an information traffic jam or overload commonly results in more directives being issued by top management. This in turn creates a lack of confidence among mini-company members and begins a vicious circle. However, the responsibility for overcoming such problems remains with the mini-company members. They are the ones who must ask "So what?" to clarify issues so that their actions can be tied to objectives, customer satisfaction, and mission. Acquiring such skills is an important part of achieving their destiny.

Here are the key questions relating to setting up the objectives and scoreboard:

- Have clear objectives been set to tie the mission to customer satisfaction?
- Is there a scoreboard with specific targets for each key objective?

- Is progress monitored to provide adequate feedback to people?
- Is there a brief explanation to highlight key issues so that people can act upon them?
- Are people interested in what is on the scoreboard? Why?

Again, information on the scoreboard or glass wall should be self-explanatory, enabling members of the mini-company to make judgments and focus on the key issues. To facilitate this, color-coded charts or charts with comments will help accentuate the message—for example, good is green, and bad is red. If the display is not well organized, it typically means either the person in charge is not clear about it or he may be monopolizing the information. In that case, whoever has the strongest need should take the initiative, raise the issue, and act upon it. If this is still not done, it is a sign of serious trouble, as there is no clear way established to expose the key problems.

Key Messages
- What gets measured gets done.
- Information needs to talk to us in order for us to act on it to add value.
- We need to understand the game we are playing.

Collecting Information

Care must be taken in handling information. The idea is to collect the information directly from the point of action instead of waiting for it to sift through several layers of the organization. Information that is directly obtained provides a sense of ownership. Since all data are collected at the point of action and transmitted from there anyway, such raw data may also be used for managerial purposes. This is an important part of developing an intelligence network. Direct contact to the source of information helps people to be better familiarized with the situation and to hone their senses as well.

Of course, certain information is still needed at the top or staff level for auditing purposes. We just need to realize that this can create layers of organizational structure and reverts back to the old command-and-control hierarchy. By using their ingenuity, however, the members can find ways to operate mini-companies with the information they collect from where the action is.

Key Messages

- Look at the reality as much as possible instead of an interpretation of reality.
- Understand what is really behind the numbers.
- Direct contact with the source of information helps to hone our senses.
- Put the intelligence where the action is.

Chapter 3

Operating the Mini-Company

❖

Good practical experience is needed to become a master. In fact, as a master in any field will attest, this is a never-ending challenge. Just reading about it is not enough. You have to go out and do it. Nevertheless, I hope the following pages will stimulate you to explore what your vision of a mini-company is.

Like chapter 2, this chapter includes questions for readers to ask themselves, or perhaps for bankers to ask their mini-companies. Some readers may feel uncomfortable without more specific instructions but I urge them to go through this exercise. Even if no clear answers present themselves now, I am sure that over time we will find the answers. In other words, to master the art of management, we should become good at questioning and answering processes between the brain and the heart, as if we are playing a game of catch effortlessly.

Problem Solving

Problems are opportunities. All members of a mini-company have to work collectively to solve them. Because of the varied nature of problems a mini-company has to deal with, we will not discuss the techniques of problem solving here. However, we should be able to answer some key questions.

- What are the major problems or concerns of your mini-company?
- How do you know that they are the major problems?
- What is your approach to solving them?
- Do you have the requisite tools and abilities to solve them?
- Do you have a strong desire to solve them? Where is the proof?

Since objectives and the means to achieving them may be confused sometimes, it is helpful to imagine a cascading structure. The higher-level objectives leading to accomplishing the mission are at the top. Layered below are the factors that contribute to accomplishing the objectives. Each of these factors in turn will have another layer of factors representing a cause-and-effect relationship for the whole (see exhibit 3.1). So if we are to be effective, we must sort out the major problems on which we need to focus. Also, it is important to represent this visually so that the focus is not lost while other people can contribute their ideas.

Exhibit 3.1
Clarifying the Key Issues of the Mini-Company

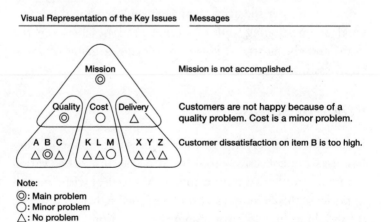

Visual Representation of the Key Issues   Messages

Mission is not accomplished.

Customers are not happy because of a quality problem. Cost is a minor problem.

Customer dissatisfaction on item B is too high.

Note:
◎ : Main problem
○ : Minor problem
△ : No problem

In this exhibit, if we are asked to identify the main problem, we may say, "It is the customer complaint, B." But, we must be prepared to support this statement by saying, for example, "Our key objective in accomplishing our mission is to work on quality, cost, and delivery to satisfy our customers. As shown on the scoreboard, our major problem is quality. Then, we can see from the chart, the number-one problem is the customer complaint on B."

As obvious as this may seem, if we are not careful, do we not find ourselves too involved in working on noncritical issues, like the items A, X, or Z on this exhibit, instead of addressing the main problem? Not just at work, but in our life in general. We have to guard against becoming too attached to certain emotional issues instead of putting our energy to a more productive use. This is why we ask, "So what?" and why we practice glass wall management: to expose areas of concern. It may be obvious in concept, but we must raise our awareness and realize that we have a choice—even to detach our negative emotions. We need to practice this diligently and continuously.

As previously discussed, just knowing how to swim in concept does not mean that we can really swim. A good test is to picture whether a stranger can determine that what this mini-company is doing makes sense. In other words, he should be able to see how this mini-company is "swimming" in business, solving problems and showing results that are undeniably good. We can further imagine ourselves visiting the mini-company as auditors to determine whether what is supposed to be happening is actually happening.

Key Messages

- Problems should be exposed clearly in order for people to act upon them readily.

- Whoever has the most pain should take the initiative to relieve the pain.
- Ask the right question over and over. If we keep trying, eventually we will discover a solution.

Addressing the Problem at the Source

It is important to address a problem at the point closest to where the action is. Needs are often felt first at the operational levels. Where possible, action should be taken there rather than waiting for top management to discover the problem and initiate action. An analogy here is using a personal computer instead of the mainframe computer to solve a problem. Even if there is a need for top-down action, the hierarchical approach does not necessarily bring out the genuine initiative and potential talents of people. We need to utilize the intelligence that is spread throughout the company and let people there do the job as best as they can.

This also means that every person in the company needs to try to delegate his or her job as much as possible. Whether it is in problem solving, decision making, or any other management task, the principle is the same. To do this well, however, the tools or approaches people use should be customer friendly. Just as the user friendliness of the personal computer and web site design have been the key to bringing more opportunities to people worldwide on the Internet, the effectively decentralized management can be realized through minicompanies. It is not a question of whether we can do it. It is a matter of when and how.

Here are the key questions relating to delegation and resolving problems at the source:

- Are you trying to solve problems by yourself or letting people do their job? Any examples?

- Do you see people taking ownership to solve problems on their own? Why is it so?
- Are you trying to eliminate your job by delegating as much as you can?
- What action are you taking to delegate more and to educate people?
- Do you think it is possible that you could be the main stumbling block in promoting self-management? If so, what can be done?

Remember that knowing and doing are two different things. We need to go beyond answering these questions conceptually. We need to see the evidence of our specific actions, and to use this evidence as a mirror to know ourselves better. If we do this with other people, we may start to learn more about ourselves. We can do this alone by having a quiet time to reflect as well.

While I was touring the factory of a large automotive manufacturer in Illinois with Gary, the vice president of operations, we saw an operator doing the monotonous job of sorting parts. As we watched, I asked Gary if he could picture this man at the dinner table that night when his son asked "Hey Dad, what did you do today at work?" If we were he, how would we respond to that question? If his father thinks of his job only as a way to earn money, how will this little boy visualize his own future? All managers must look beyond the directive to increase productivity and confront the most fundamental issue of all: to utilize people's creative potential and not treat them like robots.

We do not need sophisticated techniques to figure out the kind of problems we have. We simply need to open our eyes and ears and listen to the message coming from our workplace. If we are in the position to influence other peoples' lives, we must offer whatever assistance we can to develop their creative talent. Perhaps we should see them as customers, with whom we can share our vision. We should also provide the right tools and create an environment in which they can grow. We should guide them and help them solve problems. People at the front line can also be presidents of their own mini-companies.

Key Messages
- Address the problem where the action is.
- Our job is to eliminate our job.
- What they have not learned, we have not yet taught them.
- What we see in the organization reflects the mind of the people there, especially the mind of management.

Developing and Executing Business Plans

As problems are identified, plans of action should be developed to address them. Whether we call them business strategies, business plans, projects, or suggestions, they serve the same purpose. Many plans may need to be developed and followed through. Still, we need to clarify the process as much as possible. The ability to integrate and orchestrate all plans with a clear focus indicates our level of management ability. We need to be clear on who is to address what problems, and when, where, why, and how (5W1H).

Here are the key questions related to business plans:

- Which business plan is most crucial in accomplishing the mission?
- How can you prove it? Can you demonstrate the relationship of key business plans and their impact to accomplishing the objectives?
- Does each business plan address who is to do what, when, where, why, and how (5W1H)?

- How do you review progress?
- Is the linkage between the plans and objectives clearly displayed so that it helps people to communicate and work together to implement the plans?

When we are very much involved in a task we spend too little effort evaluating how it fits into the total picture. Our hands may be moving but we are not using our brain. Or we may be using part of our brain effectively but not reflecting on the overall picture. We must be able to prove that the approach we take makes sense in the overall scheme of things.

The questions above should help us do this, and provide evidence of our own ability to follow through with good management discipline. Someone who can answer these questions easily and produce supporting evidence quickly is likely to have a good sense of the process, and good execution and follow-up skills. If we cannot answer these questions readily, it most likely indicates uncoordinated management practices that need improvement. We must see that the total picture is not just for the president of the mini-company to understand but for the members as well.

Some years ago an experiment in Japan used the game of go to examine how the human brain functions in developing strategy and executing it. A professional "go" player's brain was studied while he played a game. Go is a complex traditional Chinese game of strategy to capture the territory on a nineteen-by-nineteen matrix board. The chief finding was that this player used his right and left brain alternately in developing strategy and deciding on the best moves. This means that to develop the best strategy we need to use more than just logic, or our left brain, to determine if a move is correct or not. We must also use our intuitive sense, or right brain, to see if that move fits into our overall strategy.

In our *organizational* setting, we must go through the same process to clarify the strategy by asking these questions of ourselves and our staffs. Again, this is like playing a game of catch. In a *personal* sense, this is like playing catch between our brain and heart. The better coordinated this process is, the more coordinated our management process will be. In the mini-company setting, "playing catch" can be extended from the individual to the mini-company to the larger company and even to society. By everyone participating in this process, therefore, we can create an interesting prospect to find the destiny for all.

Bill, a VP of sales, ran a mini-company in a medium-sized California company. When he left to pursue his own interests, his replacement found that his mini-company was so well organized that the transfer of the job went very smoothly. The new VP commented, "It would have taken many more months to catch up if Bill had not practiced the mini-company idea."

Kevin, a production manager of a Taiwanese company which won a Deming award, said, "Before we practiced the mini-company concept, we had binders of information scattered all over. In a way, it was like they were assembled for someone else like my boss and staff people to manage my job. But after practicing the mini-company for a while, I created a single binder that captured all of the information critical to running my company. I can answer any questions about my mini-company anytime. On top of that, I spend much less time accomplishing what I did before. By the way, it is not just for my benefit. The glass wall we developed consolidated the key information so that everybody can check it and discuss ways to solve problems. Everybody is involved and it is a great place to work."

Both of these managers were uncertain about introducing the mini-company at first. But after seeing others in their companies practicing it and gradually trying out the idea, both of them were sold on the concept. I believe the mini-company can work anywhere, whether in the United States or any other country, in sales or manufacturing, at the top or lower level of management, or in a large or small company or in government.

Key Messages

- Well-organized information helps to focus on critical issues.
- Develop a comprehensive nerve system to clearly link objectives and business plans.
- By using such a nerve system, problems will be exposed for quick remedial action.
- The mini-company works and brings benefits in virtually all settings in business and in life.

Developing the Heartbeat: PDCA

As we execute our plan, we need to check the progress at certain intervals to see if further changes are needed. A series of steps called PDCA (plan-do-check-act) provides the feedback necessary to adjust our course. Whether we are climbing the mountain of our dream, launching a rocket to Mars, sailing across the ocean, or running a business, the PDCA cycle should be followed. Just as our hearts rhythmically pump blood throughout our bodies, our organization needs the heartbeat of the PDCA cycle. It is like providing a spark to ignite the engine at certain intervals to assure the progress. When applied across the organization, this is like tuning and timing multiple cylinders—mini-companies—to get the maximum output from an engine to reach the destination.

Depending on the situation, however, the frequency of PDCA may vary. Strategic and longer-term projects may have a quarterly cycle. More routine activities are done daily or weekly. Whatever the case, we need to establish this heartbeat within each individual and at every level of the company. As PDCA rhythm is established and fine tuned, a sense of effortlessness, ease and momentum will develop. I will explain later how PDCA is tied to creating the mini-company annual report or having a shared event.

If the basics of PDCA are not followed, people are likely to behave in a haphazard manner which we call PDPD (plan-do-plan-do). In this climate, people become shortsighted, trying first one thing, then another. There is typically no accountability and no effort to make the most of what we've learned. This frequently happens because bankers (bosses) fail to monitor the learning and growth of the members of the mini-company. It may be difficult to convince bosses to change their behavior. Still, everyone needs to implement the PDCA cycle in his or her area of responsibility.

Key Messages
- Every organization needs a heartbeat.
- PDCA is the engine of the organization. It provides the basic feedback and learning mechanisms to move the company forward in accomplishing its mission.

Progress Reports

Summarizing progress is like assessing our appearance in the mirror. It offers an opportunity to answer "So what?" questions in an organized fashion. Whether monthly or quarterly, the progress report needs to explain clearly what the mini-company has done to accomplish its mission. It should share both good and bad experiences, lessons learned, and propose actions for the future. It should also demonstrate how the wisdom of the mini-company is captured and resources are utilized.

We may list accomplishments or acknowledge that certain problems are not yet resolved. We go beyond just listing numbers from the scoreboard. The progress report should reflect a sense of ownership and, at the same time, analyze the trends in the chart and evaluate our operation from what we call a "zero-base." We should also incorporate feedback from others, sharing it not just with bankers and members of our mini-company, but also with customers and suppliers where appropriate. Just like the glass wall, the report should be self-explanatory to get the point across.

In summary, the major benefits of writing and sharing a progress report are:

- Writing helps to organize our thoughts with objectivity.
- Understanding what happened and why will guide us better into the future.
- It clarifies the mini-company's business for bankers, suppliers, and customers.
- It provides a checks-and-balances process for monitoring progress.
- It offers an opportunity to review people's ideas.
- It provides a forum to display accomplishments and a sense of ownership.
- Regular preparation of the report helps develop a PDCA heartbeat.
- The progress report is a milestone on the journey of the mini-company and its members.

A table of contents for a mini-company progress report might read as follows:

- Name of mini-company
- Mission statement

- Mini-company profile
    Names of members and their skills and background
    Customer-supplier relationship
    Products, services, process outline, competitor profile, etc.
- Objectives and trends in performance indicators
- Status of business plans and their relationship to performance indicators
- Accomplishments (with examples)
- Lessons learned
- Existing problems
- Plans for the future
- Requests for the bankers

If this list seems too comprehensive for a mini-company in the early stages of development, a briefer report could focus on key points such as (a) what went right and wrong; (b) why; (c) lessons learned; and (d) future plans.

Progress reports have to be self-explanatory. Here are key questions related to the progress report:

- Do you review the effectiveness of business plans with bankers and members of the mini-company at certain intervals? How meaningful is that process?
- Does the report talk to those people? If there is a unique point for attention, is that noted on the chart? Is the cause-and-effect relationship clear?
- Is the report easy to understand? For example, are colors like red and green used to highlight the point on the chart? Is the idea of management by exception exercised to focus on the key issues?
- Does it cover what went right and wrong, why, what lessons were learned, and what actions are to be taken in the future?
- Does the report answer the question "So what"?

Key Messages
- Establish a heartbeat in reviewing progress.
- Good organization and objectivity are keys to identifying issues.
- Make the progress report self-explanatory. Add intelligence to it.

The Mini-Company Annual Report

An extension of the progress report is the annual report. This is highly recommended for a number of reasons:

- The annual report may encompass the annual budget and business plans as well as individual performance appraisals.
- The annual report provides an opportunity for longer-term evaluation of progress.
- Reviewing the annual report is like a game of "catch" between the banker and the mini-company president. It helps complete company-wide business plans in a form suitable for evaluation.
- The annual report is in effect a resume of the mini-company president and its members. This helps to promote their sense of ownership.
- Like the progress report, it is a way of displaying accomplishments that might otherwise go unnoticed.
- It is an important additional step in accentuating the PDCA cycle.

Here are a few stories related to publishing a mini-company annual report:

About five years ago a successful multinational mini-company at a major German manufacturer started to prepare its own annual reports. These people, who represent twelve different nationalities, have been proud of their success. The report included charts and pictures, which communicated the progress in a very comprehensive manner. When the parent company relocated most of their operations abroad, I was not surprised that this mini-company was allowed to remain in Germany based largely on the evidence provided by their annual report.

A Dutch mini-company was created on a trial basis and at the end of their first year prepared an annual report. The author of the report, an operator named Corry, concluded it by summarizing the following accomplishments:

- We analyzed problems ourselves.
- We executed improvements ourselves.
- We used support and staff services on our own initiative.
- We organized and managed our daily and weekly meetings.

After the president of this mini-company presented their report to top management, they decided to implement the mini-company idea division-wide. Now the total division of two thousand employees is run by forty-six mini-companies, each guided by a self-assessment checklist covering areas such as teamwork, communication, attitude, leadership, growth, performance, and various control activities including quality of work and organization. These mini-companies have become a showcase for visitors from other divisions who come to study what can be accomplished simply by tapping into people's potential.

Mario, a production manager in a mid-sized California company, told me that when things are not going well, he goes back to read his annual reports which recount many accomplishments. They remind him that progress does not necessarily follow a smooth path. He rejuvenates his energy by reflecting on past accomplishments and redoubles his efforts to continue the journey. In that sense, annual reports can be like base camps on our climb to the top of the mountain.

Key Messages
- Annual reports bring out pride in our accomplishments.
- The annual report serves as a resume of people and their achievements.

Bankers' Role

To help the mini-company accomplish its mission, the bankers or bosses should meet with the president and mini-company members on a routine basis to clarify all critical items discussed up to this point. This will help make the most of everyone's talent. Remember that bankers are also mini-company presidents for their own area of responsibility. The bankers' relationship to a mini-company president is essentially the same as the relationship between the mini-company president and his or her members.

In summary, here are the basics of the bankers' role:

- Set the guidelines and rules of the game for the mini-companies to play by.
- Let mini-companies play the game.
- Let them grow based on their own initiative as much as possible.
- Provide guidance and resources as needed.
- Protect mini-companies from outside disturbances. This will enable them to focus on their critical activities.
- Delegate responsibilities where possible to encourage mini-companies to grow.

- As mini-companies grow, focus more on future strategic issues.

In practice, bankers should:

- Ask questions as appropriate.
- Encourage people to find the answers themselves.
- Provide knowledge or skills to the mini-companies as needed.
- Identify areas to help, give guidance, and provide necessary support.
- Be humble. Learn from people.
- Walk the talk. Practice what you preach.
- Encourage making key information visible on the glass wall and show how to use it.

Bankers must listen to what the mini-company is saying instead of just telling it what to do. If the mini-company president is a chronic complainer who does not take the trouble to back up his or her complaint with real evidence, the banker must show the president how to address issues with supporting logic. Again, the process is like playing a game of catch or applying the dialectic method of questions and answers. Bankers are customers receiving feedback on the status of business or suggestions. But they are also suppliers providing guidance or guidelines. Bankers should try to get to the core of issues by asking, "So what?" Yet during the discussion, they also must listen to the message from the heart. Ideally, this question-and-answer process has been anticipated by the mini-company president. In other words, he should do the homework.

Key Messages
- Bankers need to clarify the game that the mini-company plays, then step back and let them play the game.
- Bankers must ask the right questions and guide the mini-company president as appropriate.
- Bankers should cheerlead and enjoy sharing in peoples' growth.

Bankers' Meetings and Mini-Company's Meetings

The bankers' meeting may be held weekly, monthly, or quarterly, depending on the need. Where possible, it should be held using the glass wall where key information is displayed on the scoreboard. Progress reports should be also prepared and shared. This facilitates a clear focus and flow in the presentation. Typically, mini-company presidents make their presentation following the structure of the progress report mentioned before.

Here are the key points to keep in mind for the presentation:

- Supply hard data and facts. Use the glass wall.
- Illustrate what you say and support it with evidence.
- Information presented should be self-explanatory.
- Focus the presentation on key issues, i.e., practice management by exception.
- Use charts to illustrate past performance.
- Explain the relationship between the trends on the chart and business plans that influence the results.
- Show examples of plans that worked and those that didn't.
- Explain lessons learned.
- Describe what is expected in the next period.

- Propose issues that bankers need to be informed of for them to take action.

Bankers should follow these guidelines:

- Encourage the mini-company to follow the outline above in their presentation.
- Show the mini-company president how to improve his or her presentation.
- Make sure that the linkage among plans, objectives, customer satisfaction, and mission is clearly established.
- Ask the right questions. The ones provided throughout this book may help.
- Provide specific instructions for growing specific areas of the mini-company.
- Acknowledge the efforts and accomplishments of the mini-company members. Share the pain that results from unresolved issues.
- Propose new ideas for consideration.
- Discuss plans for the future.
- Encourage taking on further challenges.

A bankers' meeting brings a heartbeat to the organization. Where appropriate, other mini-company presidents, members of mini-companies, customers, and suppliers should be invited. Instead of vertical one-to-one communication between the bankers and the mini-company president, such an open setting provides checks and balances as well as opportunities for mutual learning.

The PDCA cycle of monitoring progress and sharing learning is the heart of the matter. It should deal with changing conditions of business. The PDCA cycle should create coherency and clarity throughout the organization. It should follow a sequence of fact finding (check), analysis (act), development of plans (plan), and execution (act), over and over. The feedback and checks and balances that this system offers will bring about the gradual evolution and upgrading of the mini-company's operation.

The mini-company's own meeting is a reflection of the bankers' meeting. If we substitute "mini-company" for "banker" in the discussion above, we see the same relationships: bankers to mini-company presidents and mini-company president to the members of the mini-company. The difference may be the frequency of the meetings. If the bankers' meeting is held monthly, for example, the mini-company's own meeting should be held more frequently, perhaps weekly. Also, task forces, committees, and project teams should follow the same structure so that the total operation of the company can be managed by the same principle.

Key Messages

- Hold a meeting to report progress, exchange ideas, make judgments, and recognize efforts.
- The better prepared and organized the presentation, the more focused, and the more value is added at the meeting.

The Mini-Company Open Day

Typically, open days are held yearly after the mini-companies complete their annual reports, involving everybody in the company. The idea is mainly to share accomplishments, promote mutual learning, and show appreciation for everyone's efforts. It can often be like finding hidden treasures of the company with fun and pleasant surprises.

The principal activity at the open day is visiting the various mini-companies and exchanging ideas, as people do at trade shows. Hosts may use visual displays or glass walls to show visitors how their mini-company has been running. They typically display performance trend indicators, actions taken, benefits accomplished, and examples of successes. Annual reports are available. Visitors may ask questions and discover things that were not obvious before.

In addition, more formal presentations may be made by selected mini-companies. Top management may reflect on the year's progress. It is basically an open, stimulating experience for all to appreciate the year's accomplishments. Various awards may be given during this event. A typical format of open day is as follows:

- Opening remarks
- Visits to exhibits
- Presentations by mini-company presidents
- Award ceremony
- Closing statement

Some people display videotaped annual reports on open day. These tapes may mix humor with a serious presentation of performance highlights, using specific examples that can sometimes bring smiles and a sense of appreciation from the audience. Generally speaking, people want to do a good job of sharing their experiences, so they prepare thoroughly for open day. Often suppliers or customers of mini-companies want to exchange ideas on these occasions so it creates an environment to share everybody's creativity.

Open day provides an opportunity for everyone to check the progress of each mini-company. Companies may also conduct surveys and publish the results to encourage further progress. The "open" nature of open day may make some people feel uncomfortable. But my advice to those that feel this way is to adopt a positive attitude. You will probably feel much better as soon as the day's events start. Remember, we must learn to trust each other in good times and bad.

Just like the glass wall, the open day reflects our progress. Even though we are busy, we must pause to prepare the annual report. Then we share that in the bankers' meeting. After that we stop the company, say, for half a day for the open day. By exchanging ideas with others we enrich our life experiences. It is the occasion to appreciate the efforts, and renew our spirits and energy.

Depending on the size of the company, the open-day concept may be implemented in stages. For example, we can begin with a local open day, expand it to a regional one, and then to a company-wide open day. Or it can be timed to coincide with a company's other major functions. Exhibition, presentations, and recognition are the key components of the structure. Openness and voluntary sharing are the key attitudinal prerequisites. Like anything else, however, our heart should be in it if we want to see real success. If the company has no such event, a mini-open day can be developed. After all, it is a question of our own initiative.

Key Messages
- Have a moment to cross-fertilize ideas, stimulate our minds, and recognize our efforts.
- Don't just rush around trying to get things done. Take a deep breath, look around, smell the roses, "listen with your eyes open," and clap hands for a job well done.

Awards and Recognition

When we look back on the most memorable times at work, they are often events that connected people. These occasions are not always joyful. Sad occasions touch our hearts too. But whether or not we derive a sense of *meaning* from our work may depend on whether we feel deep emotion at certain times. Numbers on paper are not everything.

I remember a company with a thousand employees in Malaysia that installed "cake meters" at the end of each of its production lines. When people met their targets, they celebrated by eating cake. In Austria, a company posted a mascot bear on the wall to represent the monthly award for the best-run mini-company. A 150-employee California company developed more than a dozen award programs for employees. At the other extreme, I visited a company that did not even recognize an employee with a fourteen-year record of no absences. And there are still many companies that have not instituted a workable suggestion program.

These examples highlight the mind-set of managers toward *people*. What is at issue is whether we can make work a meaningful experience. We must recognize accomplishments and share them with everyone. It is a question of being genuinely human.

Logic may tell us that recognition is insignificant compared to making money. But is that really so? Can we hear a different voice coming from within? What if there were no occasions in life that touched our hearts? Recall the beaming smiles of children after they have accomplished something—perhaps learning to ride a bicycle or answering a teacher's question correctly. Isn't everything expressed in those smiles? Best efforts were expended, and something was accomplished. So, we smile and celebrate the occasion. Is it not that simple and natural?

If there is no awards ceremony, we can create one. One of the most memorable moments in life may be that we can reflect on some event in our past when we did our best and were proud of it. That is what brings additional meaning to our lives.

Key Messages

- Take a moment to reflect.
- Have an occasion to recognize the best efforts.
- Have a sense of compassion.
- Numbers on paper are not everything.

The Mini-Company President's Role

The role of mini-company president should encompass all the "basics" of the mini-company operation that we discussed previously. As we also mentioned, the banker's role toward the mini-company should be analogous to the role of the mini-company president to his or her members. Let's condense the roles of the mini-company president down to the essentials as follows:

- Create the vision.
- Collect the wisdom of the members.
- Encourage initiative.
- Develop an environment to foster continuous growth.
- Share and confirm the strategic direction.
- Ask the right questions.
- Use the brain.
- Listen to the heart.
- Live with the mission.

The president of the mini-company should have a stronger devotion to accomplishing the mission of his mini-company than anybody else. If this is not the case, the mini-company idea will not work. If the president has to struggle to maintain his or her dedication, he or she should consider it part of the journey and well worth the effort. This goes with the sense of ownership. As the sincere efforts become more widely known, more people may want to start mini-companies in their areas too. Thus the whole company will be activated, creating a truly dynamic and lively organization.

There will be times when the struggle seems endless and we may doubt our own capabilities. Perhaps we will feel too weak to take on additional challenges. Or we may hear a voice whispering negative thoughts that cause us to lose confidence. Yet if we reflect on past accomplishments, or ask the "So what?" questions, I am sure that we will build a foundation for the journey ahead. Individually, we all go through these crises. Collectively, we can help each other along on this journey.

Key Messages

- The mini-company president should identify himself with the mission.
- Without the spirit, there will be no creative ideas generated nor will we connect with people.
- Use the brain. Listen to the heart. Live with the mission.

Principles of Mini-Company Management

Comprehensiveness and clarity have been emphasized repeatedly because they lead the way in developing organized thought processes. For example, we will be called upon to explain our critical business plans and whether they are ahead or behind schedule. If we cannot do this, we have to ask ourselves why. We must have a clear idea of the status of all the key projects. Otherwise, even if we expend time and energy, if it is not a critical job the outcome may be quite disappointing.

The PDCA cycle and the mission are engines to ignite us to move forward. On the other hand, the customer-supplier relationship, objectives, and business plans constitute the *principle nerve system* we need to develop and work on continuously. It is fundamental to managing any business. This should be fully ingrained in everybody's mind.

In summary, the principle of managing mini-companies is as follows. "We have a common mission: for the business to be successful. To achieve this, we need to satisfy our customers. Accordingly, objectives are developed. To accomplish these objectives, we develop business plans and execute them to solve problems. To assure progress to accomplish our mission, we produce progress reports that are reviewed at the bankers' meeting. Whenever we can, we share our learning and show appreciation for everyone's contribution toward making our mini-company successful."

Because of its importance, I'll repeat this in a different order: "Developing and executing business plans enables us to solve problems of importance. By doing this successfully, we achieve our objectives, which in turn satisfy customers, and hence achieve the mission of the mini-company. To assure progress, we develop progress reports and share them in the banker's meeting. Whenever we can, we share our learning and show appreciation for everyone's contribution toward making our mini-company successful."

If we review the "Basics of the Mini-Company" in chapter 2, we see that it reflects the key principles described in these statements. Ultimately, every mini-company should practice this by involving all of its members. If this seems too obvious and simple, it is meant to be so. Utilizing peoples' full potential is the key to building the backbone of management with an organizational nerve system.

Key Messages
- Create a backbone in management.
- Comprehensiveness of information is the foundation to bring new insight.

- Comprehensiveness helps collect the wisdom of people.
- If we are concerned that a mini-company will require a tremendous time commitment and a diversion from day-to-day operations, remember that engaging the brains and hearts of people will add to the value of their efforts.

Chapter 4

Tying Things Together

❖

Mini-company management may seem complex because of its encompassing nature. But the basic approach is simple. If we want to master it, it is the *practice* that we need to pay attention to more carefully.

Mastering mini-company management may seem different from learning to ride a bicycle but both processes are based on acquiring skills. They both correspond to building a neuron network associated with personal experiences. Mastery of any subject may be seen from such an angle. It is about understanding how we use our minds and developing an environment to effectively practice a discipline that makes sense. This demands both time and energy, as well as patience.

In this chapter, we will look into overall management processes, glass wall management, and creativity. This should help to further synthesize ideas about the mini-company and integrate them into a broader dimension.

The Roles of the Mini-Company

Each mini-company serves a variety of functions for its own members, bankers, customers, and suppliers. Also, each mini-company plays the role of customer, supplier, and banker, or members of a mini-company from the perspective of another mini-company. If we look at it from the broader viewpoint, as shown in exhibit 2.4, we find that every mini-company is a part of a convoluted network of business processes similar to the elements of a neuron network.

What this means is that a "self-centered" approach cannot work. It causes disruptions in the total system. For example, if a mini-company is very demanding of suppliers and at the same time does not listen to customers' feedback, it is self-contradictory. When a banker is very demanding of its mini-companies and at the same time it is not a practicing mini-company itself, it is self-contradicting as well. The process must be *reciprocal* in order for the whole organization to function on an integrated basis. As we talk, for example, we also need to listen. Awareness of this fact has to become the foundation of our behavior, which we call our conscience.

When such conscience prevails throughout the organization, the whole organization can function effectively like a well-coordinated soccer team or symphony orchestra. It may be compared to the evolution of a democratic society from a dictatorship. If we cannot achieve this coordination, we may have to go back to the traditional or autocratic way of management.

Key Messages
- A self-centered approach causes disruption in the functioning of a totally integrated system.
- Do for others what you want them to do for you.

An Overall View of Mini-Company Operations in the Company

I mentioned that mini-companies exist at all levels of the organization. Each manager of a division, department, section, or unit is seen as a mini-company president. While a division may be called "macro" and a department might be "micro," depending on the scope of responsibility, conceptually they function in the same way as a mini-company. The relationships among the mission, objectives, business plans, and progress report across the company is shown in exhibit 4.1.

Exhibit 4.1
Relationships among Mission, Objectives, Business Plans, and Progress Reports across the Company

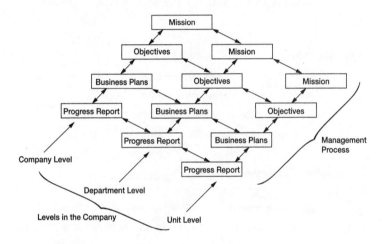

Note: At the higher level of organization, business plans may be called a strategy. At the lower level, they may be represented by tasks and SOPs (standard operating procedures).

As shown here, the linkage across organizational levels should be maintained by connecting the key management processes of mini-companies such as mission, objectives, business plans, and progress reports. Coupled with a mini-company's customer orientation, the bankers' meeting coordinates activities to assure linkage in both vertical and horizontal directions within the organization. Just as our brains will not function well with broken neuron linkages, everybody should assure that the linkages related to his area of responsibility are securely established.

As I will describe later on the topic of glass wall management, this linkage has to be clear to everyone in the organization. Just as all soccer players should know the rules of the game and where the ball is at any given time, this notion is important to expose any major problems in the organization. To develop a healthy company, each mini-company must (a) practice good management principles, (b) assure its links with other mini-companies, and (c) practice its problem-solving capability.

Key Messages
- We need to develop and practice coherent management processes throughout the company.
- We need to expose problems by practicing good management discipline to collect the wisdom.

Process Control in Management

In business, the game is played according to business plans. Just as any software company's products are programs for customers to use, we need to develop and execute intelligent programs for our companies to function. These may be called a corporate strategy, business plans, or standard operating procedures (SOPs). Collectively, they represent the core intelligence of the company. SOPs are used to keep the process stable and to allow us more easily to identify the root causes of problems. When the problems are resolved, SOPs are upgraded.

How successful we can be will depend not only on how these programs or ideas are created and executed individually, but on how they are integrated. We must be able to assess the situation, come up with ideas, sort them out, prioritize them, and execute the ideas into action. This is the PDCA cycle again. We need to reflect on what we have learned so that we don't make the same mistakes repeatedly. Furthermore we must strive to create something unique and workable that enables the organization to accomplish its mission. A company's competitiveness is the result of such collective efforts.

Since there are many issues to be addressed in a company's operation, effectively exposing problems becomes critical in order to take the necessary action in a timely manner. For example, critical quality problems should be exposed on the glass wall using key performance indicators. Then we should look at the business plans that are related to improving the quality performance. Here, we may see several plans in different stages of development. Some may be on schedule (green) while others may be behind schedule (red). So we must try to figure out the relationship between business plans and performance indicators in order to decide how to reallocate resources. We also might facilitate the implementation of certain plans or come up with new plans to address the problem.

This is common sense. Yet, as more projects are introduced to address various challenges, we may lose the total picture and work on low-priority items without realizing that more pressing problems should be addressed first. Therefore finding ways to effectively expose problems is imperative. The same thing happens in our personal lives. We may get bogged down with minor details and end up losing the bigger picture. For this reason, we have to constantly clarify issues and focus on the most critical problem as we saw in exhibit 3.1. As obvious as it may seem, we have to develop good *habits* in practicing this—*individually and collectively.* Otherwise, we may be rearranging the deck chairs on the *Titanic* when the ship is about to sink.

Exhibit 4.2 below illustrates a specific approach to assuring that we address the critical issues. Here, quality, cost, and delivery are selected as objectives to accomplish the mission of this mini-company. We can see a problem relating to quality as shown on the scoreboard. By studying the relationship between objectives and business plans, we can see that plan A and plan C have been developed to achieve the target on quality. Plan A is expected to contribute more toward achieving the target on quality than plan C. Then we see that plan A is on schedule and that plan C is behind schedule. By studying the status of performance indicators and their corresponding plans this way, we should be able to figure out the relationship among them and to adjust the plan or devise a new plan to address the problem.

As we said earlier, a well-run mini-company behaves like a well-performing soccer team. Everybody knows where the ball is. Everybody understands how they fit into the total picture. When this is the case we can tap the collective wisdom of people to come up with ideas to solve problems or adjust the plans for better performance. By condensing the whole mini-company operation into an exhibit like this and posting it on the glass wall, everybody can see how working together will achieve the common purpose. Visually displaying such relationships and continuously using them contributes to building the strong backbone of management.

Key Messages
- If we cannot clarify which issues to work on and why, whether in business or in life, we are vulnerable to being controlled by irrational emotion and becoming lost in the turbulence.
- We need to develop a strong backbone as the core of managing our business that everybody can identify with.

Exhibit 4.2
Example of Linkage between Mission, Objectives,
and Business Plans

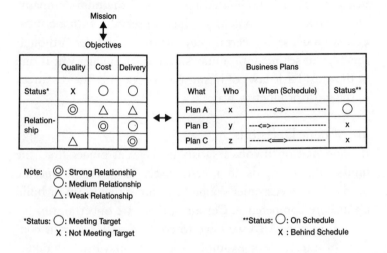

Note: ◎: Strong Relationship
O: Medium Relationship
△: Weak Relationship

*Status: O: Meeting Target
X : Not Meeting Target

**Status: O: On Schedule
X : Behind Schedule

Note: There are various ways to visualize the relationship between objectives and business plans. This is one example. Whatever way we choose, the point is to be able to identify what action results in what measurement and on which area to focus our attention to address the problem.

Strategic Considerations

As middle management becomes more involved in strategy to meet today's business needs, upgrading the strategic awareness of middle to lower management becomes more critical. Covering a wide range of strategic alternatives is not the main purpose of this book but a brief mention of three areas may help to accentuate the focus in this direction. (For more discussion of mini-company strategy, please refer to chapter 7.)

Segmentation

Just as asking "So what?" will help to clarify things and maintain the focus on key issues, the idea of segmentation helps to channel the limited resources of the mini-company. Here, the idea is to look at products or services with a critical eye. We must satisfy certain key customers first. Even though this type of segmentation may sound discriminatory, it is one of the most basic laws of business to fully utilize the resources in the most productive way.

Investment Decisions

If segmentation involves satisfying key customers first, the mini-company needs to invest wisely to meet the specific needs of these customer segments in order to sustain or build up its core competence. Certainly, there are uncertainties for any projection. Also we have to contend with inherent conflicts of interest. For example, some of our various bankers may focus on financial returns, others may p͏ more empha-sis on reflecting the change in customers, c͏ h-nology, or regulation. The challen͏ ss that incorporates different consid͏ ci-sions that emerge can be justified n. Here, combining an analytical ap ive approach is needed to make a soun gle criterion exclusively can be very ha

People

The process of developing strategy is essentially a matter of people working together and sharing their learning to come up with strategic insight. Organizational learning has a lot to do with the performance. If people cling to obsolete ideas in a fast-changing industry, the mistake may be costly. Examples may be (a) a mini-company may narrowly pursue its own interest, and (b) it may lack information about how to capture customers, while competitors, technology, or regulatory atmosphere may be changing. Ultimately, the ability to respond to the change depends on the people within. Overall mini-company performance rests upon relationships between peers. There should be an explicit process to engage people.

↑ explicit process

In the last few sections, ~~we~~ mini-company manageme~~nt~~ roles of the mini-company and strategic needs, we c~~an~~ processes. The idea is to ha~~ve~~ while utilizing people's speci~~al~~ not the same as doing. We need ~~to~~ practice this across the company—continuously. From my experience of working with numerous companies around the world, I cannot emphasize this point strongly enough. The whole process needs to be clear to everyone's eyes to assure the integrity of the whole operation. This leads to the next important subject: glass wall management.

Key Messages

- Developing sound strategy requires continual prodding, coaxing, and exploration.
- It is not just the content of strategy that is critical. Involving the people in developing and executing the strategy is equally critical, if not more.
- Sound strategy matches the needs generated by the changing business environment with the organization's strengths while covering its weaknesses.

Glass Wall Management

If we contrast a hierarchical top-down approach of management to the needs-driven customer-oriented approach of mini-company management, they may be compared to a centralized large frame computer and a decentralized network of personal computers. The hierarchical approach has its role. Yet because needs are captured better at the operational levels, we should utilize intelligence, which is spread out across the company. In exhibit 2.4, we referred to such organizations as neuron type organizations in which problems are addressed wherever the need is felt. It may be compared to having a small government or small-sized headquarters and letting mini-companies manage their own business. For such a vision to materialize, however, top management's proper guidance is required.

Glass wall management can make a tremendous contribution toward realizing our vision. The idea is to make the business process visible and comprehensive so that, as we said before, even strangers can understand what is going on without asking questions. The idea is simple and it enables us to focus on the critical issues. For example, everyone should be familiar with the company's strategy. But if that strategy is not explicitly captured on the glass wall, obsolete patterns of people's behavior may easily hamper progress. Also, without the clarity of glass wall management, determining what or why certain things must be changed depends on subjective or intuitive judgment. As the pace of change accelerates, depending on such judgment becomes increasingly unreliable. These points highlight the strategic importance of practicing glass wall management.

Glass wall management is comparable to accessing web sites on the Internet, where ease of access and rich content are critical attributes. It is also like having an open mind as opposed to a fixed mind-set and an inability to see the broader picture or to utilize our hidden talent effectively. The problem I found in visiting many companies is that while most of them collect vast amounts of information, it is neither well organized nor used effectively. In other words, this information did not provide answers to the "So what?" question and other key questions raised in chapters 2 and 3.

When we practice glass wall management, what is understood is visible and easily utilized. As more people become accustomed to mini-company operations, a conducive environment is created where people will help each other accomplish the mission. Even if nobody actually encourages you to do this, I still believe your own conscience should encourage you to practice this idea.

Exhibit 4.3 shows an example of a mini-company practicing glass wall management in their meeting area. The Basics of the Mini-Company, including mission, objectives, business plans, and progress reports are displayed and used as a part of the regular meeting of the mini-company. To assure that the basics are practiced, each and every mini-company should have a setup like this whether it is at the shop floor level in manufacturing, in offices or hallways at the human resources department, or in top management offices. The information is exhibited where the action is, and can be communicated to anyone visiting the area, including bankers, suppliers, and customers.

Exhibit 4.3
Glass Wall Management Practiced in a Mini-Company
Meeting Area

• Mini-Company Annual Report
• Monthly Business Report
• Meeting Minutes

Key Messages
- Capture the intelligence where the action is.
- Listen to the message with eyes open.
- The mini-company and glass wall ideas are to be integrated to create a dynamic organization.
- Glass wall management helps to cross-fertilize ideas autonomously when it is tied to the initiative of the people.

The Self-Organizing Process Using the Glass Wall

As more comprehensive management information becomes available, greater cooperation among those interested in the success of the mini-company becomes possible. For example, with the glass wall, a customer visiting the supplier's mini-company may develop a better understanding of the state of the projects underway. Members of the mini-company are able to receive quick feedback on their performance. Someone passing by may notice a lack of progress in a certain project and make a suggestion to that project's owner, or may discover a nice presentation of data and "steal" that idea to use in his own mini-company. Bankers also find the glass wall useful to cross-fertilize success stories among the people. The accumulated results of these are a build-up in the capability of the whole organization.

Glass walls are used in mini-company meetings to share progress and ideas. As people go through such a process repetitively, a shared understanding will be developed among the members. Glass walls may also be used in bankers' meetings. By sharing key information and following up, bankers develop a better understanding of the operations of mini-companies. The glass wall is like a meeting that is always in progress. It provides a platform for exchanging information continuously. As discussed before, the glass wall may also be used at mini-company open days.

Glass walls promote mutual learning and idea generation while enhancing teamwork and communication. Using the brain as an analogy, this is equivalent to extending the neural network among those involved and activating the intelligence in the company. It is difficult to predict all of the possibilities of such a self-organizing or cooperative process without prior experience. But that is precisely why we need to promote glass wall management.

In my experience, the potential benefit is tremendous. Even though a certain discipline is required, it is exciting and fun. Wherever the glass wall appears—in a small or large company; in Europe, Asia, or the Americas—more comprehensive information is spread throughout the company. Information is exchanged autonomously and in a nonlinear fashion, instead of only in the conference room with a limited number of participants. After all, such open and entrepreneurial behavior is what today's companies need to cultivate. Many people are interested in participating in such a process. This may be even compared to the widespread acceptance of the Internet.

The way information is organized and shared on the glass wall reflects the personalities of the individuals involved. For example, someone may provide feedback by drawing a smiling face with a comment like, "Good job! Thank you all!" Another may draw a sad face when performance is not satisfactory. Cartoons and pictures add flavor to our work life while drawing people's attention to critical issues. We can also see how capable management is in organizing and using information. Some people may still prefer to share information verbally. Others may still think that reading the numbers in a meeting is the job of management. But without a visible display to bring out the total picture, people are easily sidetracked, lose focus, develop a biased view, or simply forget about what was discussed. If we are serious about wanting to run a business efficiently, we cannot afford that. We need proof of good management that even a stranger can understand.

Key Messages
- Let the charts speak to us.
- Let self-organization take place by involving people.

- Realize that the solution exists within ourselves.
- The glass wall shows how we are capturing intelligence.

Showing the Reasons for Existence with the Glass Wall

To check the soundness of management when I visit a company, I often ask "What is the reason for your existence?" My typical questions are: "What is most important in your area of responsibility?" "Why is this important and how can you prove it to me?" "What other areas are also important and how do you prioritize them?" "What plans of action are you working on?" "How do I know if your plans of action are truly addressing the objectives?" I do this across different levels and different functions to assess the health of the total organization, much like a doctor diagnosing a patient.

Corresponding to these questions, a glass wall should show the "proof of management" and the "reason for existence" visibly right at the site of the mini-company. The glass wall should provide a way to answer "So what?" and other key questions for people, allowing them to move *forward*. In essence, by just walking around the company, we should see what we shared in exhibits 4.1 and 4.2 related to mission, objectives, business plans, and progress reports. The key issues should stand out without spending a lot of time and unnecessary energy to bring them to light.

Exhibit 4.4 below illustrates a glass wall for company-wide concerns. Here, we see an integration of performance indicators and the business plans associated with them. Anyone in the organization can see which performance indicators are green (OK) or red (not OK), which business plans are green (on schedule) and red (behind schedule), and their relationships, that is, what causes what. This is a way to practice managing by exception so that we can focus on the critical issues instead of wasting time on low-priority items. Also, this display summarizes key issues without requiring people to sit through presentations in various meetings to figure out what is going on. It also helps us to study the cross-correlation among different performance indicators and business plans needed to capture the dynamic nature of business.

So, if any visitor can identify the key points of operations easily with such a display, then people in the company should be able to do the same—or better. Then, they may refer to their own mini-company's glass wall to see how it can contribute to company-wide concerns. Or the president of a mini-company may communicate to the members of his mini-company the strategy and his concern using such visual means. After he has explained the situation at regular meetings, people will find the visual tools helpful in contributing their own ideas for the benefit of the total organization. In this way, the backbone of the management becomes firmly established and practiced.

Exhibit 4.4
Example of Glass Wall Management
for Company-Wide Concerns

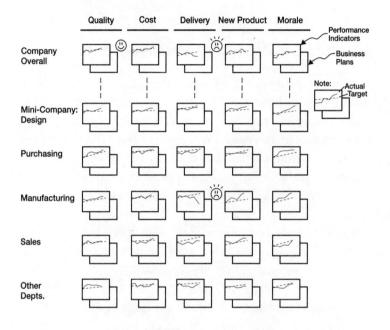

Note: Please note that staff functions like quality, finance, materials, product management, and human resources may check on quality, cost, delivery, new products, and morale respectively to expose problems and recommend actions. This corresponds to the vertical view of this display for checks and balances. For example, quality staff will check the quality performance of Design, Purchasing, Manufacturing, etc., to identify the major area of concern on quality for the total company and offer necessary advice.

Key Messages

- A glass wall shows the proof of management.
- A glass wall is a mirror reflecting our actions and what is in our mind.

- Glass wall management helps to transfer management skills more easily.
- Glass wall management helps to integrate company operations.

Benefits of Glass Wall Management

Running a mini-company is directly tied to the mastery of what we do in business. The glass wall presents a visual display of what we practice and provides feedback to keep us on the right course. If we cannot organize information and make key information visible, that typically means our minds are not clear on the topic. So what is or what is not on the glass wall indicates what is and what is not the focus of our attention.

Coupled with the mini-company idea, therefore, practicing glass wall management helps us to identify areas we need to work on. In summary, here are the benefits:

- Provides feedback on the status of business, exposes problems, and identifies areas of focus quickly.
- Forces us to be fact oriented.
- Develops pride as clearer understanding is gained, and shows the evidence of how things are managed.
- Breaks down territorial boundaries. Helps to develop teamwork.
- Facilitates open communication.
- Encourages us to achieve the common good.
- Helps develop an intelligent nerve system within the company.
- Helps to check the overall health of the organization.
- Helps to hone our senses in assessing the state of business.
- Promotes better resource allocation and speedy action.
- Brings fun with creative displays.

- Helps people to grow.
- Provides an environment that promotes a self-organizing process, i.e., bring out the creativity of people.

The glass wall provides an environment that facilitates interaction among people. However, for it to produce benefits, it has to be tied to people's initiative. The benefits do not come overnight. It requires a commitment to developing the management process and everybody's ability to *effectively* use information.

Of course, displayed information should be current and relevant as opposed to, say, posting information because the boss said to do so. The aim is autonomous management and problem solving. The glass wall confirms that important principles are practiced and evidenced. There may be moments of embarrassment when the glass wall does not look good. But there are situations for pride, stimulation, and learning as well. Because the glass wall is intended to promote a self-organizing process, a shifting of emphasis from hierarchical control to a needs-driven approach is necessary. This requires a change in attitude, behavior, and habits.

Key Messages

- The glass wall promotes the self-organization process.
- The glass wall reflects the mind-set of management.
- As good athletic coaches use the blackboard to illustrate how strategy can work, the glass wall provides a means to share critical concerns, thereby developing the backbone of management.

More Consideration of the Bankers' Role

As mini-companies develop, bankers must redefine their own roles just as parents need to change as their children grow. As the company grows and management becomes more complex at the top, it is entirely possible that communications can get out of hand. The answer is for the CEO to direct top management to practice mini-company ideas so that they themselves can benefit from glass wall management. As obvious as it may be, the CEO should ask top-level mini-companies to demonstrate the reasons for their existence. Total integration of mini-companies can only happen when the CEO practices these ideas on his or her level.

There are cases of having multiple bankers for a single mini-company. For example, in a matrix-type organization bankers from both line and staff functions may oversee one mini-company. If so, it is important to have a clear platform where these bankers can meet and agree on plans for allocating resources following the example in exhibit 4.2. It is not difficult to allocate resources if all the key people are there to discuss the total picture. This is contrasted to having separate meetings, say on quality and cost, or by products and regions.

Lack of coordination among bankers can result in mini-companies receiving conflicting signals, as if multiple coaches are giving conflicting instructions to a soccer team during a game. I call this the "cross-fire syndrome." This is the reason for creating a platform like the one mentioned above. It may take time to become good at this process of coordination. But with the help of a comprehensive glass wall, and with repeated practice, it can be done. In the meantime, the mini-company needs to develop a capability to present its case to the bankers in a very concise manner.

Key Messages

- The CEO needs to practice the mini-company idea in order to create a coherent management process for the total organization.

- A platform should be developed to resolve the cross-fire syndrome for smoother operation of mini-companies.
- Resolving problems with multiple dimensions will require high-level management capability. But since the mini-companies are most affected, each mini-company should take initiative to organize the information and make a proposal to the bankers for resolution.

Bringing Out the Creativity in People

Ultimately, business success depends on how effective a company is at developing its people's potential. Here we will investigate the process of idea generation, or inspiration, so that we can tie management practices directly to this important topic. Coming up with a good idea is like finding the *right combination* of 5W1H (who is to do what, when, where, why, and how) like completing a jigsaw puzzle. In fact, life is basically a continuous challenge to solve problems creatively to bring out the meaning in the process.

For example, what we do in thinking is chain words together so that they express something of value when composed as a sentence. A book comprises chained thoughts on a larger scale. An idea is typically a combining of seemingly unrelated items in a manner that produces a new meaning. Companies also do this by chaining processes from idea generation to design and production to delivery to create value for customers by finding the right combination of resources. Business strategy, business plans, or suggestions represent such intelligence. And finally, our civilization represents the results of all of these combinations having occurred over time. In short, I see creativity as coming up with the unique combination of resources to bring out a new meaning.

In nature, all living species go through this creative process as they evolve. In our own lives, whether it is a thought, an idea, a report, product, or service, the process of creation is pretty much the same although each of us may attach a different meaning to it. If we search for the core of this process, we will find what may be called *life energy*. Here, we find that we, ourselves, may be the most amazing creation made out of the dust of the universe. Then, our initiative or willingness are forms of energy trying to find ways to connect ideas and resources to create values that we appreciate. This is the point where the life of a man and the life of a business have a common foundation.

The question is how to bring out the creativity or hidden potential residing in each of us. Since creation is one of nature's best kept secrets, we cannot describe exactly what happened in Newton's brain when he saw the apple falling. Yet we may be able to characterize the climate in which creative ideas are born. Then we may attempt to provide such an environment. Since there is a close connection between what we see in our surroundings and our concern for developing our organization and ourselves as individuals, let us first examine what is around us, especially in nature. Here are the *characteristics of inspiration:*

There is need.
Whether we call it an awareness of a problem or life-threatening danger, there is a need to be filled. In nature, we see such situations are found in homeostasis where wounds are cured, or a group of ants fixing up their home which was broken by the storm. In our case, we try to come up with solutions, and conscious effort is required before the solution is found. Examples include running extremely fast when chased by a bear, or fighting cancer with a positive attitude. Competition, compassion, or interest brings out extra energy.

We become one with the problem when the need is paramount.

No artificial force is applied.

The process of creation is related to a voluntary action. It follows nature's way. So, inspiration may be considered a form of the self-organization process. When we cannot solve a problem, typically inspiration comes from an unexpected source. It also frequently derives from combining seemingly unrelated items. Inspiration generally comes not right after the efforts are made but some time later when we are not thinking of the problem—perhaps while we are dozing or daydreaming, or when we are in bed, taking a shower, or driving the car. The brain may be in the alpha wave mode. My typical experience is, ideas walk to us, or talk to us.

For example, dreams can bring a solution. Ants fix their home even if there is no apparent leader to give orders. Ideas are God's revelation. The tail of a lizard regenerates after it has been cut. We carry heavy things from a fire without realizing our strength at the time. Children play with toys.

Sufficient resources are provided.

In the case of homeostasis, living cells around a wound self-organize to fix the wound. In our case a large amount of memory is stored in our unconscious that can be activated and combined to provide ideas or possible solutions to problems. Life on earth was born out of a certain combination of events and materials to find higher state in chaos.

For example, memory cells in our brain combine to create something new, just as interaction of people with various backgrounds generates ideas. A curious person finds even ordinary things unique and of great interest.

Inspiration comes suddenly.

Solutions are often realized unexpectedly. They may be traced back logically later. However, sometimes the logic is unclear and the solution is seen as pure luck. There may be a triggering event, such as a falling apple, or a bright star in the early morning. Stimulation or new information often triggers a solution that we know intuitively is the correct answer. It just happens. We may realize that the solution has been within us for a long time, just waiting for the right moment.

For example, the sound of a crow awakens a Zen monk to enlightenment. All of a sudden, a child discovers how to ride a bicycle. The moment of "Aha!"

There is joy in that moment, and a feeling of confidence.

The more difficult the problem, the greater the joy when its resolved. It makes us feel jubilant like touching the core of our existence. It may create a long-lasting memory and influence on our life.

For example, whether the moment is memorable or not, examples may be found in experiences of almost everybody. We see it in a child's smile.

In summary, inspiration shows up when the need is felt. Yet it happens not when the efforts are being made, but when we are not consciously striving for it. In order for it to happen, sufficient resources must be provided to form a solution. When it happens, typically it happens suddenly. Then we understand intuitively that the solution is the right one. Often, a logical explanation follows, confirming that it is the right solution. At that moment of inspiration, we experience a great joy.

Inspiration is a moment where our life energy channels through us and moves us up to a higher state. Inspiration means a connection between our brain and our heart. Here the heart expresses our life energy and the brain provides the logic to follow the laws of nature. An inspiring experience can bring the sense of our total existence beyond words. It can make any one of us feel genuinely happy and appreciative.

Key Messages
- Creativity is nature's process.
- Every one of us appreciates having such a moment.
- Creating an environment that fosters creativity is an important part of every manager's job.

Creating an Environment That Fosters Creativity

By studying interactions between organizations and individual motivation, we can build on the discussion above to create an environment that fosters creativity. For example, we can create inspiring moments with awards and recognition or encourage the self-organizing process with the glass wall or open days. Thus, developing strategy or mastering tools, or becoming leaders or entrepreneurs may be seen as ways to express our creative nature. So following our previous discussion we will try to provide such an environment.

There is need.
The mission of the mini-company represents the need. Specifically its customer orientation highlights the need to come up with plans. The glass wall stimulates people to focus on specific areas, thus exposing needs for more people to address. Every day conscious efforts are made to address issues of concern. The bankers' meeting and progress report also accentuate the areas requiring more attention.

No artificial force is applied.

As mentioned previously, a mini-company is needs driven by virtue of its own initiative. Within the mini-company, entrepreneurial behavior and the voluntary nature of actions are encouraged. This emphasizes the need to connect genuine desire and listening to our heart without preconceived notions. The glass wall is where the facts are displayed. Here the organized information provides a basis to explore new ideas.

Sufficient resources are provided.

There is a rich source of information on the glass wall. There are also stimulating events like mini-company open days or open forums for brainstorming sessions. Such an environment opens up various ways for people to interact. By utilizing intelligent information, the potential for idea generation is enhanced and situational leadership and entrepreneurial behavior are encouraged. As more people join and information becomes more accessible the effect increases exponentially.

Inspiration comes suddenly.

As more people see the potential of the mini-company, they become interested in exploring their own potential. Running a mini-company has elements of a game using a scoreboard or a glass wall even though the business itself remains serious. As we explore the "game," eventually there is a moment of discovery. Everybody was once a child and can relate to that experience. When the glass wall is kept somewhat informal, what I call a "kindergarten effect" may take place. Cartoons, pictures, or balloons on the glass wall introduce an element of fun and attract more people to participate in the game.

There is joy in that moment, and a feeling of confidence.
As more people share their success by putting their stories on
the glass wall, even more success is generated thus creating a
stimulating learning environment. This may even lead to
what is called "organizational enlightenment" where a whole
organization is activated and realizes a sense of oneness—just
like we may find at certain sports events. Thus a dynamic
organization has materialized from people's own initiative.
There should be a sense of fun and movement in the air.
Remember, however, that this process has no end if the
organization is to continue to thrive.

In summary, practicing mini-company principles in the glass
wall environment fosters a self-organizing process. This in
turn brings out people's hidden talents while enabling us to
master the tools necessary to find our destiny. Mini-company
open day, customer day, use of the Internet, and participating
in a users' group are other approaches that will help. All
mini-company presidents should cultivate such an environment.

Last but not least, voluntary help is a form of creativity as
well. It is an expression tied to the sense of oneness. When we
see someone in trouble, we want to help. When our brains
are not making much noise, we may identify the pain of others as our own. When our colleagues receive awards, we join
in the celebration. This is a self-organizing process where
there is no pretention, only genuine desire. *Compassion* flows
from the heart—the flip side of wisdom or creativity. Even
though modern life may obscure things if we are not careful,
the basic nature of humanity should not be forgotten.

Key Messages

- By understanding human nature, we can create an environment that fosters creativity and addresses basic needs.
- The organization needs to develop a setting like the mini-company and glass wall management to explore ways to express everybody's potential.
- We will find basic human nature expressed even in the days of modern management.

Chapter 5

Getting Ready for Implementation

❖

Here we will show how to use tools, techniques, and concepts as opposed to being used by them. We will also discuss leadership and entrepreneurship as ways to express initiative. Even though mastery is only realized by actual practice, studying these subjects should assist us in developing our individual and organizational capabilities.

Again I realize that these topics may seem intangible or elusive to some, but readers are reminded to read this book with their *brains and hearts* to grasp the essence. Remember also that awakening and inspiration may come only after *deliberate and conscious efforts* are made—not immediately after we study the material.

Top Management's Roles

The CEO should also be a mini-company president for his area of responsibility. He or she should practice the same basic discipline as the others. Although the CEO may have less time for reflection, he or she must *answer* all questions that were raised for the mini-company in chapters 2 and 3. The CEO should also ask these questions of his staff to assure the integrity of management in practice. Top management needs to then develop a comprehensive management system utilizing such means as a bankers' meeting, open day, and the glass wall.

"Policy management" is an approach that assures that the whole organization is focusing its energy on critical issues and that the heartbeat of PDCA is present. The CEO should go through the cycle of review in the bankers' meeting using charts like exhibit 4.4. Even though top management may not *control* total operations, they must be able to clearly describe the critical issues of the business and have a mechanism to assure that the organization is functioning to address them. If they cannot, that is the worst kind of problem an organization can have. Practicing the mini-company idea at the top will help address this point and enable the CEO to be master of his destiny himself.

Here are key questions for top management:

- Do you practice mini-company ideas in your areas of responsibility?
- Do you put yourself at the level of your people/employees to review and assure the integrity of the total management system?
- Is there a good checks-and-balances system developed and functioning?
- Is the whole management process comprehensive enough for even strangers to understand?
- Does your genuine inner desire match what you practice at work?

Of course, these questions apply to all mini-company presidents too. We also need to ask "Where is the proof?" or "Show me the reasons for your existence" so that we are operating our business on a firm foundation.

When management loses its initiative and lacks the ability

to demonstrate the reasons for its existence, chaos tends to prevail and the backbone of the company disappears. In such a case, top management and those in staff functions tend to revert to the more traditional mode of "managing" or "controlling" instead of "coordinating" and "fostering" ownership for mini-companies.

Of course, when children are not yet grown up, parents have to do the work for them. Yet their efforts may also backfire, as children may never have a chance to gain the necessary skills to discover their hidden potential. A similar situation can prevail in the work environment. If they lose their own initiative, bosses and staff people may suddenly start dictating orders without a coherent effort to coordinate among themselves, suggesting that problems have not been solved where the action is. A traffic jam of information at higher levels of management frequently causes added headaches while obscuring critical issues in the process.

Some may say that such chaos or confusion is a fact of life. My recommendation, however, is to strike a balance between the urgent job and the important job, and to allocate time and energy accordingly. An urgent job may be to practice mini-company ideas in order to focus on the key issues. On the other hand, the important job may be to let everyone acquire the necessary skills to grow with mini-company ideas. In short, top management should put their efforts into developing the backbone of management and practice the idea of the mini-company across the whole organization.

Key Messages
- The organization reflects the mind of its management.
- Management needs to place themselves at the level of their people to review and assure the integrity of the total management system.

Middle and Lower Management's Roles

The mini-company idea applies to everyone whether they are at the top, middle, or lower levels of management. Learning and growth opportunities exist at all levels and for everyone. A common language and common principles enable communication to be much more streamlined resulting in fewer information traffic jams. In contrast, the more traditional, hierarchical approaches in business offer much more limited learning opportunities.

Since middle- and lower-level managers are the top management within their own mini-companies, they should do their jobs before complaining to others. In fact, if we ask "So what?" in response to complaints, we need to realize that in sailing or in business, whichever way the wind blows, we need to trim the sail and steer the rudder to reach to our destination. Each of us must develop the ability to find our own destiny.

The nature of the wind may differ somewhat between top-, middle-, and lower-level management, though the basic setting is the same. Some think that talking to the wind may help, even if this makes no sense. The bottom line is that each of us must ask "So what?" or "What can we do about it?" Then we should manage as best we can to focus on critical issues and refuse to be disturbed by the noise. We have to work on this skill repeatedly. It ties to the notion of making people, i.e., developing sound managerial capability in each of us.

Key Messages
- We cannot direct the wind, but we can adjust the sails.
- Instead of complaining to others, let us figure out what we can do. Life does not wait.
- Sort out the noise and focus on what is essential, i.e., the mission.

- The bigger the noise, the more we need a strong will, sincere desire, and a cool head to seek the right course.

"Making People"

As discussed previously, the mini-company should develop a nerve system that can quickly sense when people need to take prompt action. Pain should be felt at the right place, at the right time and should stimulate the person with a strong initiative to respond. The simple rule that applies here is: "No pain, no gain." From mission to objectives, from customer feedback to project execution, the deviation from the expected should be exposed. Then problems are prioritized, and actions taken accordingly. The glass wall helps to accomplish this in another way I call "management by embarrassment" or "management by conscience." People will take action on their own initiative because nobody wants to be embarrassed by seeing his area covered with red on the glass wall. It is an issue of conscience. This is where we find the connection between the organizational nerve system and each individual's initiative.

A self-initiated drive for betterment can help a person grow more than anything else. Then, as problems are exposed on the glass wall, we may also willingly offer help to whomever is in need. This is like the tug from our heart that motivates us to take action for a good cause, which leads directly to the idea of making people before making products or services. If we believe that this scenario is impossible—for whatever reason—most likely it will become so—limiting our own potential growth as well. This is because the interest to make it happen is already missing at the starting line. But, if a dream touches our heart, we may hear the message "It is well worth the effort."

Achieving the mission requires a constant effort—even a

struggle. This is a fact of life. But that effort makes us appreciate the fruit even more. To help understand this process, exhibit 5.1 shows how we can move forward in our journey, accomplishing our mission one step at a time. And as we build our experience base, we gain more insight and skill in running the mini-company.

Exhibit 5.1
Overcoming Hurdles to Accomplish Our Mission

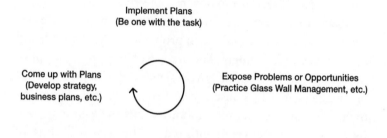

Implement Plans
(Be one with the task)

Come up with Plans
(Develop strategy,
business plans, etc.)

Expose Problems or Opportunities
(Practice Glass Wall Management, etc.)

Solve Problems or Capture Opportunities
(Bring out the insight)

This is essentially the same as the PDCA cycle explained earlier. Propelling us to grow with every cycle is like having an engine for the organization that exposes problems or opportunities. It acts as a spark to initiate the cycle, signaling us to take action. So, the *heart* is where genuine desire and initiative are found. Our *sensory system* identifies problems and opportunities, while our *self-organizing* process produces solutions, and *action* allows us to execute business plans.

In exhibit 5.1, solutions to problems are translated into plans for execution. They represent the key intelligence of a business as summarized below:

- *Mission:* Reason for existence, purpose.
- *Strategy:* Critical approaches for the total organization to accomplish its mission.
- *Business plans:* Plans set and agreed upon to get the job done at all organizational units.
- *Tasks:* Typically short-term projects set by individual units or task forces to address special issues.
- *SOPs* (standard operating procedures): Procedures identified to assure the integrity of the operation.

Here, the basic elements of who, what, when, where, why, and how (5W1H) have to be clear. After execution, we must follow up to continue the PDCA cycle. Each cycle should bring new learning and insight, which can be incorporated into the next challenge. A company that lacks the nerve system to identify its needs and is unable to create a vision, approach, or learning process, is like a pilot flying a plane without instruments, adequate skills, or a map to rely on, and with no clear destination for the journey ahead.

Key Messages
- Make people before making products or services.
- Provide a system to expose the pain.
- Whoever feels the pain should take initiative to address the needs.
- Without effort, there is no progress.

Finding Congruency

One way to evaluate the performance of a mini-company is to check the degree of congruence among the president of the mini-company, its bankers and members, and others related to its operation. Is the mini-company's operation adding value to the organization at large or focusing on the suboptimization level? Is it run by professionals with integrity, or run by a few individuals who are imposing their own personalities on it and not relating to others?

In short, this is about the personal bias we find in any organization where some influences are stronger than others. We need to guard against the concentration of power that limits the expression of a broad range of opinion. We must maintain objectivity while producing insights to enable the organization to go beyond the influence of limiting viewpoints. Without mechanisms to insure objectivity and the opportunity to capture the maximum talent of the organization, the aspirations of a few people will dominate.

There is a big difference between the president of a mini-company who asks "What do *I* want to accomplish?" and one who asks "What should *we* try to become?" The former is not a shared aspiration and is not supported by the checks-and-balances mechanism, that is, the interest of members, customers, and bankers.

Congruency is a question of matching self-interest with the interests of the organization. This is why it is important to involve all members of the mini-company in creating its mission and to use glass wall management and bankers to perform checks and balances. Accepting assistance is not synonymous with sacrificing leadership. In fact, creating the mechanisms for assistance as described in this book is one of the most important challenges for any manager. It is essential to develop the *insight* to resolve problems associated with issues of congruency. In essence, this is equivalent to learning to see habitual ways of doing things in a different light. Instead of confining our thoughts so that we fail to see the broader picture, we need to understand different viewpoints and listen to our hearts so that we can gain insight in finding the passage ahead.

Key Messages

- We need to work on matching self-interest with the interests of the organization.
- Accepting assistance is not synonymous with sacrificing leadership.
- Let us develop the setting to collect the wisdom of people, and gain insight to find the passage ahead.

Introducing a Rhythm

We have seen that continuously going through a cycle of *exposing* problems, *solving* them, *developing plans,* and *implementing* them (PDCA starting with "check") is a way to move forward a step at a time while also building up our abilities. Here, the notion of rhythm requires attention. Day and night, the four seasons, our heartbeat, breathing, and the life cycle of living species are all examples of rhythms found in nature. Rhythm helps to bring orderliness and promote self-organization, creativity, and teamwork.

Laboratory experiments show that when heart muscles are separated from each other, each has a rhythm of its own. But close together their rhythms become synchronized. People walking together in the street or running a marathon often fall into step spontaneously. Musicians in an orchestra achieve harmony under the direction of a conductor. When a flower blooms, butterflies arrive to pollinate it. It is no accident that these self-organizing rhythms occur spontaneously.

When rhythm is developed, there is a sense of togetherness as well as a smooth channeling of life energy. While we may not be able to force it to happen, when we are in synch with the rhythm of nature we find ourselves in good spirits and better focused. Without being told, we know what is the right thing to do. Our work gets done more easily; we are "in the zone." Even our hearts and breathing seem to develop a steadier rhythm which in turn replenishes our oxygen. There is a state of oneness in what we do.

If, instead, our rhythm is disturbed, our ability to focus on a subject or organize our thoughts is negatively impacted. Typically, in such a state of chaos or confusion there is no steady rhythm and we may suffer outright shortness of breath. Then, the brain and heart become disjointed from each other. For example, Ingram, the president of a furniture manufacturing company in Georgia, spoke to this disorder by instructing all his mini-company presidents to plan their day to include one hour every morning for themselves. Only urgent phone calls would be allowed. This helped people to create quality time to develop the heartbeat of PDCA.

As in the case of the orchestra conductor, a good leader develops a good rhythm within the organization while sparking people's initiative. It is like finding the resonance or right wavelength. This cannot be completely understood by the brain but has to be experienced. Finding a real sense of rhythm should be considered a key element of successfully implementing mini-company strategy in such areas as bankers' or mini-company meetings, open days, and the annual report. This rhythm forms the essential *heartbeat* of the organization.

In summary, developing a good rhythm may bring the following benefits:

- A sense of togetherness, or oneness.
- The smooth flow of energy without waste.
- All is activated in harmony.
- A focus on the task at hand.
- Facilitation of the self-organization process.

Key Messages
- Listen to the heartbeat of the universe.
- Develop the heartbeat for the organization to move forward.

Mastering Our Tools

Our mission in action involves mastering the tools that are the means to accomplish the mission. They may be used for such things as problem solving or executing tasks. In a broader sense, money, words, concepts, or our work are also tools to accomplish something with higher meaning.

When tools are seen simply as tools they lose their connection to the mission. They also lose their meaning. This happens when we function mechanically without asking "So what?" On the contrary, the master discovers this connection and brings life to tools. He uses tools like a part of his being. As he become one with his tools, the whole entity expresses its whole potential.

If we are not masters of tools, tools may use us. Just think about riding a bicycle for the first time. Before we could ride, we were separated from our bicycle, not expressing the potential in any harmonious way. Listening to someone tell us how to ride a bicycle does not help much either until we actually try it. Yet after practicing for a while we develop the knack of riding and we become one with the bicycle. Or, at least, we are not as disjointed as before. We move our bodies without thinking to get the desired movement of the bicycle to take us where we want to go. In this way, the bicycle becomes a tool that allows us to reach our destination without much difficulty.

A similar thing happens when we run a mini-company. A "concept" may be implemented without heart. Yet the concept itself has no life. It is merely a tool until it comes alive.

The point is, it is not the form of the mini-company we are after, but a substance—a *living* proof, a dynamic state of motivated people working together to accomplish the mission. When such state is realized, resources and tools are connected in people in serving the purpose, expressing their potential, and are in good harmony. Like riding a bicycle, we should experience the state of oneness in running a mini-company with people and tools all contributing their potential.

Like brushes are to painters or instruments to musicians, there are requisite tools. We find masters everywhere in nature. Fish swim, birds fly, and spiders build their webs, for example. All their tools are fully activated. There is no waste. Even a person unfamiliar with the mechanics of flight can see that a bird uses all its resources to fly. The lesson is that mastery is achieved only when we devote ourselves fully to the mission. Only after dedicated efforts will we suddenly find ourselves in a state of oneness with our tools. When we reach this state, our brain and heart are one and we may discover that we have found our destiny. We become the destiny itself at such a point.

A master can easily distinguish whether people are using tools or being used by them. The master may provide a few pointers but he or she knows that the skills must be internalized by the beginner in order to achieve mastery. We should try to internalize the skills necessary to master one basic tool rather than attempting to master too many tools at once. If we can internalize one tool and use it with integrity, such an experience will help us acquire the skills to internalize more tools. The bottom line is that if we are to master anything, our efforts must come from the heart.

Key Messages

- Logic is a tool and needs to be linked to the heart to bring it to life.
- Ultimately, tools, our actions, and our answers to questions should connect to our heart to bring out the meaning.

Leadership: Expressing Our Beliefs

If leadership were simply a tool or technique, we could master it using programmed training. But leadership is more than that. It is also the expression of a strong belief and an inner desire to accomplish something important, in this case the mission of the mini-company.

For example, I write this book in the belief that it will help connect our work with a fulfilling life. I want to share what I have learned. If I truly believe and become one with this task, even if my command of language or other abilities are lacking, I am sure I will find a way to overcome these hurdles. I believe that life's journey is a continuation of such a process. If I live my life from the heart I may find I can be just as happy no matter how difficult the process is. Even if this book only reaches a single person, if the potential exists to share my knowledge, why wouldn't I do it? And if I find the writing difficult, so what?

Henry Ford said, "What is desirable and right is not impossible." Here "desire" comes from the heart and "right" is following the law of nature. So, we cannot be totally blind. The brain has to provide the logic as nature intended. Yet the brain must be connected to the heart to bring out the meaning. This is how leadership should be practiced in the mini-company as well. It is "situational" and connected to each individual's initiative. At the core of the needs is the origin of leadership in a form of creative power. If we listen carefully to that need which is desirable and right, such leadership is just a matter of expression of life itself.

After Soichiro Honda, the founder of Honda Motor Company, resigned as president, he visited all seven hundred Honda sites. He shook hands with every Honda employee to say thank you. Honda declared that he wanted to do that no matter how long it might take or how remote the location might be. Whether it was a maintenance operator with oil-stained hands or a clerk at a small local sales office, he shook hands happily with tears in his eyes and realized his dream after many months of travel.

Here I see a genuine human heart expressing itself and connecting with others. The expression may differ for each individual and specific situation. Still, what they have in common is a sincere desire to realize a dream. Rather than thinking of leadership as a skill that we can learn, we need to connect to the core of our being to find what we really want to express from our heart. Whether we are running a mini-company or cleaning an office, if we practice what our heart desires I have no doubt that our actions will lead to a life well lived.

Key Messages

- Genuine desire coming from the heart will somehow find the means to express itself.
- What is desirable and right is not impossible.
- People do not move because of logic alone.
- If our heart is in the right place, we can connect to babies, flowers, machines, and people without using any words.

The Mini-Company and Entrepreneurship

Tied to situational leadership, the mini-company introduces an element of entrepreneurship. Entrepreneurship can be seen as a way to express our nature as we explore the future. The mini-company president tries to create the vision, define its universe, and explore ways to accomplish its mission. Even though a mini-company may appear different from an actual start-up company, there are essentially identical elements. In fact, the mini-company concept originated in my idea that as people grew in what they did, they would prepare themselves to run a company or at least to internalize useful skills for their future. Thus, the approach became the concept of the mini-company, which, in turn, became a rewarding experience for me and I believe for those who have practiced it.

In keeping with the entrepreneurial spirit, practicing mini-company ideas can result in huge benefits if the president is willing to strike out into the unknown. To accomplish the mini-company's mission, its president may have to come up with new strategy. He or she may have to reach out to different customers or suppliers or develop different products or services. In fact, the mini-company may even find different bankers outside the company if the current bankers do not support its mission or business plan. In essence, this is the free enterprise system introduced within the company. In fact, what is also interesting here is that the mini-company can even function without the support of the company since it follows the basics of management anyway. What it comes down to is the spirit of people in the mini-company who take pride in what they do.

Some may think such entrepreneurial behavior does not conform to the company's overall goals. Yet, from society's point of view, if a mini-company or its president can find different bankers and create greater value, the total contribution to society is greater. On the other hand, if this mini-company does not fully explore its potential, that potential is lost. Just as a democratic society allows individuals to freely express their opinions, such a viewpoint may need to be incorporated in the management of today's business instead of allowing bankers to monopolize the power.

By asking "So what?" in order to think things through, the mini-company president challenges bureaucracy and company traditions. This simple act challenges the status quo, complacency, and conventional wisdom. However, this entrepreneurial spirit needs to be channeled under proper guidance. Here, the heart counsels: "Do what you believe in." From the brain, the guideline could be: "Use your common sense." And the last essential point is: "You have to prove it."

As much as some mini-companies find themselves acting as suppliers to their competitors in order to survive in a fierce economy, we need to be open to all possibilities. The creation of a new business could result from some unique combination of the mini-company's new experiences in supplying its competitor. Legal issues must be considered, but glass wall transparency, the banker's insights, and the mini-company's own initiative may make this opportunity worth pursuing. Remember that our whole society is moving toward utilizing the most of everybody's talent. The question is not whether or not we practice the mini-company idea. Rather, it is how well we practice the idea—organizationally as well as individually.

Key Messages

- The creative spirit of the mini-company may be released in the form of its entrepreneurial behavior.
- Do what you believe in, but use your common sense. Then you have to prove it
- Let's figure out how best we can contribute to society individually and organizationally by practicing the idea of the mini-company.

Principles of Organizational Development

Understanding our roles, mastering our tools, providing leadership, and being entrepreneurial are the fundamentals that need to be internalized to develop an organization that can thrive today. External needs can be met by building up our internal capabilities. To summarize the main points, here are seven steps to developing an organization, that is, our mini-company.

- We want control where the action is.
- We want to have people there contributing to their fullest potential.
- We want to provide "customer-friendly" tools for them to utilize.
- We want them to use these tools to self-manage their areas better. ·
- We want them to fully utilize their ability to come up with creative ideas, implement them as appropriate, and share the progress.
- We want them to be stimulated by what they are doing. We want them to continuously learn, grow, and have fun.
- We want to master these fundamentals so that we have time to explore on our journey.

Here "we" represents higher-level management and "they" represents subordinates. This may be compared to the family setting where "we" are parents and "they" are children. Since higher-level management has higher-level responsibilities, they may also be referred to as "them," with "we" representing stockholders or society at large. Whatever we call people, the point is that everybody needs to explore his or her potential.

To grow as individuals, we must go beyond the limits of

our field of vision. To contribute what we can along the way, *each of us* needs to practice these principles for our own benefit, for that of the mini-company, and even for the benefit of the whole society. Individual growth leads to the mini-company's growth, the company's growth, and even the growth of society. Having such vision in mind, let us review each of these points.

- *We want control where the action is.* Various tasks comprise many processes with control points before products or services are finally delivered to the customer. If these points are not under control, the organization will suffer. Business will become a futile task similar to trying to build a paper house in a storm. Therefore we must have a good system of nerves to expose the problems automatically.

- *We want to have people there contribute to their fullest potential.* We don't want "remote" control. Front-line people should be in charge of such control points. They must learn emergency repair skills and also how to take advantage of opportunities. Instead of treating them like robots, management must think of the front-line people as customers and treat them accordingly.

- *We want to provide "customer-friendly" tools for them to utilize.* The delegation of tasks, including managerial jobs, is critical. Managers and staffs must find ways to transfer their skills so that the whole organization will grow and become more competitive while eliminating waste at the same time. One of the major wastes in any company is underutilizing talent. To eliminate this waste, everyone needs to try to delegate or make his or her job obsolete.

- *We want them to use these tools to self-manage their areas better.* As we've said, if parents do not let their children grow up, the children will never learn to cope with life. Likewise, our employees must be allowed to use whatever unique talents they possess. If they do not utilize their talents, the whole organization suffers.

- *We want them to fully utilize their ability to come up with creative ideas, implement them as appropriate, and share their progress.* Certainly, people have initiative. They have talents to put to use. They can manage their own area of responsibility, make suggestions, help develop strategies, or even educate the boss. When this happens, we should celebrate their growth and think further about how to do more for them.

- *We want them to be stimulated by what they are doing. We want them to continuously learn, grow, and have fun.* As people develop their self-managing skills, ultimately they become the masters of their own destiny. Depending on the market, competition, and other factors in business, more opportunities may be found for the company to grow. If capturing such opportunities turns out not to be possible, the question of self-management will still remain a challenge. The question then is whether or not we can be masters of *any* situation.

When we master these fundamentals, we will be free to explore on our journey. We cannot take on more work than we can handle. We need to learn ways to balance our work with our capabilities. This is a constant challenge. As people grow, their managers need to reflect on their own responsibilities and find ways to expand their own horizons. Top managers themselves can easily become a hurdle if they do not grow along with their employees.

Key Messages

- Everybody is a manager and aims to become the master of his or her own destiny.
- Your work personality and your non-work personality have to be one and the same if you are going to be effective and happy at work and at home.
- Follow through with sound principles.

The Heart of the Mini-Company

As the mini-company principles reach out to all operations of the company, the changes they create in people's behavior and the positive impact on business performance will be substantial. Therefore, before we discuss implementation in the next chapter, let us try to capture the essence—the heart—of the mini-company.

Let us first review the key points related to the brain of the mini-company. The points involve logical reasoning that clarifies the critical issues of business while developing the backbone of management.

- Every mini-company president should be able to prove his reason for existence.
- The focus is on customer orientation and self-management.
- Developing the habit of continuously asking "So what?" promotes a clear focus on key issues in business.
- Speaking the common language of mini-company principles across the whole organization clarifies the management process throughout the company.
- Everyone can practice the easy-to-understand principle of the mini-company.
- Emphasis on comprehensiveness with visibility using the glass wall exposes problems better and more quickly while

eliminating redundancy and reducing barriers between business units.

- Glass wall and bankers' meetings provide sound checks and balances.
- The mini-company idea clarifies rules and provides a framework for people to play the game of business while expressing their talents.

Now let us review the key points related to the heart of the mini-company. These points are tied to the psychological or individual internal issues that relate to initiative, self-awareness, and ownership.

- The imperative to find our destiny brings a sense of ownership.
- It helps us develop clearer focus on key issues in business.
- The focus is on what we can do in whatever situation we are in. It is useless to talk to the wind.
- This awareness drives us to find the solution.
- The mission orientation drives teamwork and cross-functional cooperation.
- Practicing mini-company ideas creates an environment for each of us to find his or her destiny and meaning in our work even when times get tough.
- It encourages each individual to take initiative to best utilize his or her talent.
- It brings creativity, situational leadership, and entrepreneurial behavior.
- Through experimental learning each of us can become a master.
- It emphasizes fun and occasions to show appreciation for what we can do.

- It creates an environment in which we can express our potential.

After using our brains and listening to our hearts, we still need to reflect on our progress.

- The progress report and the glass wall represent the state of business. Looking at them is like looking in a mirror.

- No matter what the outcome, ultimately it is OK if we have used our brains and hearts as best we can.

- While the heart does not lie, the wrong use of our brain can mislead us. Our brains are like tools with accumulated memories, images, and logic. We need to carefully monitor the wrong use of the brain—from the heart.

- If we can do this, we can create a dynamic and "lively" organization while meeting our everyday challenges.

- The ultimate aim is total good for society. In the process of moving in that direction, we contribute what we can and find goal congruency in people's growth as individuals and that of our organizations.

- By working on key issues and employing a sound process, the genuine initiative of the people will open up the passage leading to our destination.

Do these ideas resonate in your heart? Does this list look too good to believe? Do you think it is do-able? Or, even if you are not sure about the details, do you feel convinced enough to give it a try? I believe it is do-able in virtually all settings in any organization. It is up to you to realize the dream. Imagination is power. If we can imagine it, we can make it happen. It is up to each of us to try. Ultimately, we should make the effort not so much to prove something to others, but for our own well-being.

All of these benefits are likely to appear in an *organic* manner as we implement the idea. It is like working on a jigsaw puzzle. Various problems become familiar and lead us in the direction of our next move. In this way we build our organization while pursuing our vision for the future. Because of the dynamic nature of business and us being the major factor with lots of unknown potential, a conceptual understanding by the book does not reveal the total picture. A more intuitive and holistic understanding will be developed as a part of implementation process—bringing, I am sure, many pleasant surprises.

Key Messages
- Our limited logic alone cannot bring out the most of what we have.
- In the end, it is the spirit that makes things happen.

Chapter 6

Implementation

❖

The particular industry we are in, company size, management style, and culture are all factors in where and how we start a mini-company, the duration of implementation, and possible pitfalls. Ultimately, however, what the reader gets out of this chapter will depend on the degree to which he or she believes the mini-company concept will work. I hope it connects to something deep in your heart. As Walt Disney said, "If we can dream it, we can make it."

Factors Affecting Implementation

Before discussing the specifics of implementation, let's look into various factors that affect the implementation process.

General
Implementation can start at the top, middle, or lower level of management. It can begin across the company as well. Because of the tremendous potential of the mini-company, company-wide implementation is most desired. However, if a company has more than 100,000 employees spread around the globe, it will require greater coordination.

If a company starts a mini-company in one unit, it should discover pretty much the same issues as it implements the process on a larger scale, or in a different function or division. Once a mini-company president gains practical experience and has discovered the benefits, he or she will most likely be able to apply this acquired skill in any environment.

Industry, Management Style, and Human Factors

The mini-company idea can be applied in virtually all industries because every organization is set up to achieve a mission. Whether it is in manufacturing or service, private or public, China or Belgium, there is no fundamental difference. The difference, if there is one, is related more to human factors such as the vision and the style of management.

If someone does not have a strong desire to make a mini-company work, it may be better that he does not start the process. A Dutch plant manager named Teake who has had much success with his mini-company says, "Do not start a mini-company if your heart is not in it." Initiative is the key to success. A possible analogy here is raising a child. It takes time and energy, but it is worth it. Those who are not fully committed to becoming parents should not even consider having children.

Size of Organization and Time Required for Implementation

For a company with from one hundred to two thousand employees, basic company-wide implementation may take two to three years. Even though the challenge will be ongoing, the basic framework should be developed in the first one to two years. In companies with more than two thousand employees and a more complex structure, implementation may take longer. Here again, a significant influencing factor is management initiative.

Use of the Internet

At the end of this book I've given the URL for my web site. I encourage anyone interested in mini-company management to stop by and exchange ideas and experiences. Just as the glass wall or open day can help cross-fertilize ideas, this web site can be used for similar purposes. In fact, the Internet is like a giant glass wall offering us a framework and platform to share intelligence. The key, again, is to take initiative and share ideas with others. The more interested and prepared you are, the more you will gain out of such experiences.

The Role of Training

Reading and formal coursework are not the main focus of training. Instead, the real training is in actual practice where we need to repeatedly ask ourselves questions like "So what?" until the principles are internalized and acted upon. Just reading this book may be sufficient to start putting ideas together and begin trying them out. Then, implementing the mini-company concept should present no major surprises except hard work, going through the cycle of PDCA, asking questions among yourselves, and answering lots of questions along the way.

Curious about mini-company ideas, many people have asked me to provide references so that they can visit companies that are practicing the idea. However, I try to discourage such visits until at least some experience is gained. Without experiencing the struggle to make a mini-company work first-hand, the benefits from visiting other companies are limited. In fact, a visit could mislead people who have not tried it for themselves. If you must see a mini-company in action to convince yourself that the idea is worth implementing, something more fundamental may be missing.

There is no such thing as a perfect mini-company. It is always in the process of creation. There are always problems and concerns waiting to be addressed and a mission to be accomplished. It is not the final state we are searching for but the journey. We are trying to create our own dream, and the act of doing this is the basis of the mini-company. It is like painting our own vision on our own canvas. We may never feel satisfied that it is completed. Ultimately, what we are after is a question of spirit and an expression of our life.

Establishing a Foundation

To repeat, we need to look at our reflection in the mirror. That is the starting point. Even after we've practiced the mini-company concept for some time, we need to go back to the starting point over and over to find out who we are and become one with the mission. By connecting to the energy within us, we practice what we believe in. Everything will be our teacher if we have a good starting point as the foundation.

Without this foundation, searching for solutions elsewhere does not help much. No matter how hard we study, we will see form and not substance. Thinking we can duplicate the benefits gained by other mini-companies without making the journey ourselves is futile. It would be like the tools using us instead of us using the tools. If we lack confidence in or knowledge about ourselves and our core problems, we may be looking for something to hang on to, like references, benefits, forms, tools, and programs. We may satisfy our intellect with them. But wait. Is this not one of the reasons we are in a turbulence of our own making? Where is the heart? Was it not the very point we raised at the beginning to question and listen to our heart?

Accomplishing the mission of the mini-company should enable us to connect to our life's mission. If we are one with the mission, it should be like channeling the flow of our life energy. Look at a flower growing at the roadside. Does it not express all it has? Without complaining, it does the best it can to accomplish its mission. What about us, then? If we visit and revisit the starting point and identify and connect with the core of our being and activate all our resources, is this not the point? Too much knowledge and too many tools may in fact shake us loose from our foundation. Our brain needs to connect to the heart to bring out the meaning, does it not?

General Guidelines for Implementation

The key points may be summarized as: (1) follow the Basics of the Mini-Company listed in chapter 2; (2) practice glass wall management; (3) ask the right questions, use our brains, and listen to our hearts carefully.

In the following pages, we will look into various ways to implement mini-companies. For example, management should develop the framework and encourage people to join. The bankers may offer education programs or on-the-job training. Sharing experiences with other mini-companies may provide stimulation. Furthermore, there may be an "orchestration process" to share learning with other companies. Ultimately, however, it is every mini-company's own creative process that makes the difference.

Of course, the vision and style of management are important. If management is autocratic or too detail oriented, for example, people will feel uncomfortable about expressing their ideas. This undermines the whole purpose. There has to be an element of fun and an experimenting spirit. And if the approach is too carefully engineered, it becomes "brain heavy." We have to be very practical. Remember that failure is not failure so long as we do not quit and if we can learn from the experience. That is the spirit we need to keep.

Where to Start?

You have already started if you are reading this book. One way to start is to practice the ideas where you can. In fact, this may be the most natural way, because nobody is forcing anyone to implement "the program." It becomes self-managed, as it should be. Of course, each individual will digest the message differently. But, if a few groups here or there start to apply ideas using their own initiative, I am sure that we will start to see some differences in the appearance of the area and the spirit of the people involved. The results will follow.

At the start, the mission of the mini-company should be discussed and clarified. The glass wall can be set up so people can start realizing the benefits of getting clearer feedback. Next, a bankers' meeting or a meeting of the mini-company's members should be arranged as a clearinghouse of ideas. Once experience is gained and the framework of running the mini-company is clarified, the exchange of ideas will become more productive and creative energy will start to flow more smoothly.

If everything has gone well up to this point, the strong desire or conscience of people may drive the implementation of a mini-company to a larger scale, thus gaining the critical mass to sustain the process. Then, it becomes a self-organizing process connected directly to the willingness of people—self-initiated, self-thinking, and self-controlled. If things have not gone well, a thorough reevaluation may be needed. Nobody should impose on anyone else by telling them what to do. Instead, people should ask questions, offer ideas, practice them, and share progress.

For example, Chia, the director of the home appliance division of a multinational Singapore company, told me how he started his mini-company. He practiced what he called "motipulation," a combination of the words motivation and manipulation. After attending my seminar, he passed around to his managers a copy of my previous book *The New Shop Floor Management*. Then, he used "motipulation" in such a way that his people "got" the idea of the mini-company and agreed to practice it. After several rounds of meetings, they collectively were able to summarize the essence of the mini-company in a few pages and used that as the basis for implementation.

Of course, the notion of manipulation is not necessarily a good one. But, just as parents entice children with candy in exchange for good behavior, if the objective is worthy, the practice of "motipulation" may be forgiven. Kim, one of this director's managers, later confessed to me that he was very dubious at the beginning. The message was too simplistic and he was not excited about it. But after practicing the idea for a while, he too became a convert. I was later surprised when he spoke enthusiastically about his mini-company experience at the company's management conference in Thailand. A few years later, they were awarded a Singaporean Quality Award.

Are You Already Practicing It?

At a medium-sized medical equipment manufacturer in Michigan, a human resources manager told me after my seminar that my ideas were easy to understand and that in fact they already practiced them at her company. In a large European bank, a group of top-level managers said that the mini-company concept was common sense, and that they were already practicing it, too. To explain the entire mini-company program in an hour or two is not easy. But even when I had a three-day seminar combined with a simulation game and a field exercise, which I did in more than twenty-five nations around the world, there was a case when a person thought he already practiced the idea. Their perception is their reality.

Since mini-company ideas are common sense, it may be natural to feel like that. And, in a setting like a seminar where the evidence like glass walls and progress reports is not present, the discussion cannot go far. Since it is the question of practice, we should go where the action is. Our actions do not lie; but rather speak for themselves. In addition, heart or conscience should be found at the core of the practice. Out of hundreds of companies I visited, there were only few that were at the advanced level.

In most cases, there is a missing link in the nerve system of management. It may be an unclear management report, or even what could be called a "broken backbone" in the management system. Common problems included the absence of a glass wall to display people's wisdom, uncoordinated action, unclear priorities, lack of a sense of ownership, lack of customer orientation, lots of tools without masters, many reports and projects but no summary to answer "So what?" questions, redundancy of efforts, and a missing linkage between top management and the people at the front line. Just tracing the communications links from the shop floor or front line will reveal a great deal about the sins of management.

If there is a perception gap and an absence of evidence, discussions become futile. This is why practicing glass wall management is critical. It provides a platform for exchanging ideas on an equal level beyond titles and organizational boundaries. Even though I do my portion of sharing throughout this book, I can't do much "motipulation" without interaction. Obviously, each reader has to find his or her own specific path and destiny. I simply ask readers to create time to look in the mirror quietly, and ask themselves pertinent questions. If this is done sincerely, I am sure an inner voice will reveal the answer.

Types of Implementation

The Singaporean case mentioned above is an example of starting from the top. Reading this book and applying the ideas wherever they fit based solely on people's initiative is another way. Still other approaches may be useful:

Without Top Management's Support

I heard a top manager in a large company demand that his division set up a mini-company without his involvement. Even though this does not make much sense, mini-companies have been known to work, and work well, without top management support. We could say that where there is a will, there is a way. But how the connection to the top can be made remains an open question.

With Top Management's Support

There are many cases where top management has introduced the idea quite effectively. These top managers are involved in practicing the ideas of the glass wall, bankers' meeting, annual reports, open day, and so on. To facilitate the process, there is typically someone to help them to oversee the program and establish a heartbeat. The organization of the bankers' meeting and the mini-company's own meeting are the most important platforms for sharing progress and discussing concerns, thereby developing a rhythm of PDCA and building up momentum. The "living" glass wall, which communicates the current status of the mini-company's operation, helps to initiate necessary actions while keeping everybody focused and fact oriented.

Just Starting on Your Own

Even if you are not a part of top management, you can still be the top management of your own mini-company. You should be able to start your own mini-company regardless of the size of the organization if your heart so desires. Remember that the challenge is how to run the business and express yourself no matter which direction the wind may blow. I have seen people from different levels of an organization take the initiative and implement the idea successfully. Many have been simply practicing ideas gained from my seminar.

Starting with a Pilot Project

If top management feels uncertain about setting up a mini-company, they may choose to take a pilot project approach. In such cases, a staff person often works with a manager of the unit to experiment with the idea before deciding on the future direction. There may also be constraints on time or staff. The liaison person may also be a consultant or college professor from outside the company.

I have seen many successful cases that have taken this approach. But like anything else there are pros and cons. One positive aspect is that the staff person can check the process carefully. On the negative side, it can become more "engineered" than self-initiated. Still, as the pilot project becomes successful, and more units are scheduled to launch their mini-companies, there are often more people interested and eager for their turn to start.

Starting from the Top and Bottom at the Same Time

In this case, the top management decides to practice the concept at the top before cascading the idea of mini-company down through the organization. This approach can make sense because before they ask their employees to practice, they practice the concept to prove that it works. I feel such thinking admirable. In any case, while the idea cascades down through the organization, an improvement team at the front line is created at the same time to prepare the people to use problem-solving tools and develop meeting skills essential for successful mini-company operation in the future.

Starting from the Bottom

Since there are more people at lower management levels and numerous operational problems are encountered there, many companies start implementing the mini-company idea at the front-line supervisor's level. Practicing the mini-company idea requires good discipline and an analytical mind to follow through, and its comprehensive approach connected with people's initiative very often brings a sea change in the organization. Some of my fondest memories are of seeing novices grow to become great managers running meetings skillfully, sharing their concerns with people, and capturing the spirit of continuous improvement. It is very important, however, that the implementation should reach to the top level of management in order to harness the benefits of full implementation.

Starting in a Newly Developed Organization, or Starting by a Newly Appointed Manager

When an organization is new or when a new manager is assigned to an operation or a company, it is a good opportunity to clarify the roles, responsibilities, and reporting structure. As the business condition becomes fluid the mini-company idea fits very well in such a situation. Because of the newness to the job, asking people to participate in formulating their mission, objectives, business plans, and the like will typically foster ownership and create the desire to manage their mini-companies.

When an automotive supplier in Indiana introduced the mini-company idea under the direction of Jim, a newly appointed vice president of operations, supervisors and their manager collectively developed a mission statement. When it was finally completed after discussion over two weeks, they rushed out of the room and proudly posted it with their signatures on it. They shared their views with Jim and his staff to kick off the implementation process. In Taiwan and in Mainland China, where two new electronics manufacturing facilities were built from scratch, they fully incorporated the mini-company and glass wall management principles from the initial planning period, going from startup to full production at a record speed. Lawrence, a young plant manager of two thousands employees in China, told me that it would have been very difficult to start up his factory without mini-company principles. It helped to have a common framework to work together especially considering that most people came from various regions in China without much training.

Hitting the Wall in Implementation

Implementation may start from the bottom and may produce significant results. Middle management may also support and practice the idea in their areas. But there are cases where the movement stops there when top management's support is missing. Sometimes the movement cannot go across functional barriers, for example, from manufacturing to the commercial area. A manager who has not taken time to analyze how a network of mini-companies will strengthen the entire company can squash the mini-company movement. When this happens, we need to accept the consequences, and do whatever we can under the circumstances. Still, even such cases should not be considered failures if people do not lose hope.

Starting across the Board

Concurrent implementation across the whole company is also possible. Even though it may require good judgment capability and high confidence in execution, such an approach has shown excellent results in a much shorter time than any other approach. If you are convinced that this approach offers a vast learning opportunity and that there is nothing wrong with trying and going through PDCA, this approach is recommended. Whether the company size is small or large, the critical factor for success is the support of the CEO. Launching the mini-company is a major strategic decision that will have a significant payoff for the whole organization.

The organization usually has to go through at least three cycles of PDCA to gain sufficient momentum to be convinced of the benefits. Just like riding a bicycle, we can gain momentum after the first few turns of the wheel are made. If autonomous checks and balances are in place, there may be less chance of hitting the wall in this approach. Like riding a bicycle, however, the process needs to be sustained. Here, a potential hurdle is that of complacency. We need to be reminded that success itself can become the reason for potential failure in the future.

Starting at Multiple Companies

After attending my seminar in Michigan, three CEOs, Jim, Ron, and Dick, collectively decided to introduce mini-company ideas in each of their companies at the same time. They got together every six weeks to review their progress and help each other. While these CEOs exchanged their experiences, their people also visited each other's companies to cross-fertilize ideas and share their concerns voluntarily.

With commitment from the top and various checks-and-balances review procedures, these three medium-sized companies all made major strides in implementing mini-company ideas in the following years. They also influenced other companies in the region who sent many visitors to their companies. A users' group was developed to share ideas, and a community college offered a course to extend the learning to people from other companies. Jim even coauthored two books on his experience.

Training Programs

There are two types of training programs: Each type—formal training and on-the-job training—offers unique benefits. In this section, we will discuss formal education. On-the-job training is discussed in the following section.

Formal training has the benefit of enabling a large group of people to go through a shared learning process. It may include classroom training, simulation games to practice ideas in a controlled setting, and field exercises for more hands-on experience. In the process, participants do not just learn the idea but are tested on their level of skills. In order to gain practical experience, top-level management may be advised to go through the training. The following are examples of training programs.

Classroom Training

Ideally, participants should read this book prior to the start of the training. This enables them to get a deeper understanding by reflecting on their personal situation ahead of time. It also avoids the possibility of losing the key message in the emotion of the moment during group sessions. If pre-reading is not possible, a brief overview of the mini-company is presented with the Basics of the Mini-Company (discussed in chapter 2). Glass wall management should be covered next. Where possible, examples of implementing mini-company principles may be presented by someone with experience. The group should also discuss the points of learning for each segment of the training, reflecting back on their personal experiences. Then, the group should summarize each segment by asking "So what?" to capture the principal point. The PDCA cycle is thus reinforced through practice at each training segment.

Knowing does not translate directly into doing. Gaining the skills of running a mini-company may be compared to learning how to swim. Classroom sessions alone are not enough. The final test is in the doing. Combining simulation games and field exercises with classroom sessions is strongly recommended.

Simulation Game

The idea behind the simulation game is to enable participants to get the sense of actually running a mini-company in a controlled setting. Key elements of focus include practicing the Basics of the Mini-Company, collecting the wisdom of people by practicing glass wall management, and simulating the mini-company's own meeting and bankers' meeting—all while having fun in the process. An example of a simple manufacturing simulation is explained briefly here. Varieties of such a game may be used with different scenarios.

Two or more teams of seven to ten people should each be supplied with staplers, staples, scissors, pencils, rulers, and about 100 pages of ordinary copy paper to make top-open paper boxes—that is, without a lid. Each team is given the specifications, i.e., dimensions and tolerances for the box and a certain production volume as a target. Participants are then asked to develop a mini-company operation, set up the scoreboard, allocate responsibility, lay out the production line, try out a prototype, and be ready for production in thirty minutes. Then the teams each run production for four minutes and deliver the output to the customer who may be the facilitator of this training. Key performance indicators should be monitored on the scoreboard and each group should make suggestions and implement them to improve their performance.

After allowing twenty-five minutes for each mini-company to make further improvements, there is another four-minute production run. By going through the same sequence for four production runs, participants practice the idea of PDCA and conduct an effective meeting by using the glass wall. Use of a storyboard for problem solving may be introduced after the third run. Then, at the end of the fourth run, each mini-company will make a presentation to the whole group. They should follow the bankers' meeting format to summarize how they set up the mini-company, what went right and wrong, examples of improvement, lessons learned, and so on. To introduce an element of fun, an award may be given to the best performing mini-company.

Field Exercise

In this exercise, participants visit a selected unit of a company to assess the level of mini-company operation and make practical recommendations. Each group may have up to ten participants visiting a specific unit of the company with a Polaroid camera. They will have about two hours to study the unit's operations by interviewing people there and gathering facts to make assessments. They may study subjects such as performance indicators, business plans, reporting structure, glass wall, people involvement, customer focus, and elimination of waste—all related to managing a mini-company.

A Polaroid camera is used to take pictures of particular points of interest. After the visit, participants organize a presentation using a flip chart to summarize key findings. Next, a presentation is made to the people of the hosting units, describing the observers' impressions and using pictures or copies of documents attached to the flip chart as evidence. It should highlight both good practices as well as areas that need improvement. Then, the participants explain why the symptoms they saw at the unit are happening, and what can be done about it. This is the diagnostic part—much as a doctor explains to the patient what might be the root cause of a problem and what needs to be done to avoid just treating the surface symptom. Finally, summary recommendations are made to help the unit move forward. In this exercise, the participants' ability to connect the idea of a mini-company to the actual practice is tested while the hosting units receive free advice from the group. The total time should be about three to four hours for one field exercise. As mutual interest grows, groups can visit each other to conduct the exercise at certain intervals. They may form a "users group" to keep the momentum going.

On-the-Job Training

On-the-job training should be done using the bankers' and mini-company's meetings as a platform to practice the Basics of the Mini-Company (chapter 2) and glass wall management. A staff member or consultant may facilitate the process. If this is the case, the facilitator should have practical line management experience where possible. He should help set up a certain rhythm by regularly visiting meetings to share insights, ask the right questions, offer certain techniques like problem-solving or effective meeting skills, and give adequate feedback. Because of his experience with the implementation of mini-companies in various areas, he may be able to coordinate activities of the overall movement. Cross-fertilizing ideas to develop a sense of mutual learning is a critical element in accelerating the learning and developing a critical mass of people who practice the mini-company idea.

If there is no staff or consultant involved, a group of managers should set a rhythm by getting together, for example monthly, and sharing ideas on implementation. The corner-stone of implementation should be, again, in bankers' and the mini-company's meetings in connection with glass wall displays. They are the engines of the movement. The bankers should be aware of the progress of mini-companies, and should try to promote the cross-fertilization of ideas among mini-companies to help create a stimulating environment. For example, they may encourage the cross-visitation of managers for mutual learning. Of course, bankers should attend the mini-company's meeting every now and then to provide support as well.

Specifically, one way to get the movement started is to go through the Basics of the Mini-Company one step at a time. For example, the first step is to ask each mini-company president to write a mission statement involving his people and to share it with the rest of the mini-company presidents, say in two weeks' time. As they share, bankers may give a few remarks to get the point across. After each mini-company's mission is clear, the second step is to ask them to draw a customer-supplier relationship chart and share that in two weeks. So, going through the list step by step, people can collectively learn the basic ideas, following the process of PDCA.

On-the-job training and education programs may be done in parallel. Here, repetition is the mother of skill. The key is consistency of the message and following the principles while providing an occasion for checks and balances. We need to focus on the reason for work and spark interest in doing what is right and desirable. The point is to develop a strong backbone in each individual to take greater ownership and pride in their work.

Orchestrating the Implementation Process

One of the keys to successful implementation is the process of orchestration. Here are a few examples. In Michigan, several users' groups in manufacturing companies share their experiences in running mini-companies. Each group contains eight to ten small- to medium-sized companies, with each company sending two or three participants. The president and key operations manager are the typical members. The idea is similar to the field exercise mentioned above. In this case, the groups visited one member company at a time every six to eight weeks to complete the field exercise with a Polaroid camera. A few facilitators assisted the groups. In short, this multidisciplinary approach helps to facilitate mutual learning. Many participants felt that the rhythm of going through this exercise helped them develop an excellent platform to generate the movement.

In France, several divisions of a large global company, each employing several hundred to a thousand people, got together on their own initiative to implement mini-companies. In this case, the human resources staff coordinated the program and operations managers led the movement. Every few weeks the group visited a different host division and practiced various modules of the program. People learned from this practical cross-visitation approach that the same concept works well in different industries. Soon, they developed a web site to share experiences. Like the case in Michigan, a few very committed people helped a great deal especially in the initial promotion phase of this program.

Similar approaches are practiced in various locations in China, Spain, Indonesia, the United Kingdom, and the United States involving manufacturers, distributors, and service companies. The mini-company open day and bankers' meeting are also ways to orchestrate the implementation process by providing sharing opportunities. Typically, attendants seem to enjoy gaining "hands-on" experience and find something meaningful and exciting in the process. Developing a good framework, genuine initiative of people, and good coordination are critical factors for successful implementation.

Each Individual Plays a Part in Implementation

Because a mini-company behaves like a living organism, running a mini-company requires integrating logical, intuitive, and holistic skills. In other words, the total implementation process is connected to how we function as individuals. If we are aware of this, I believe we will discover that not only in our businesses but in our own lives, our hearts are at the center of *all* of these activities.

Looking at each individual setting at work, we can see that one fundamental skill is linking specific issues to their strategic or holistic context. Any mini-company member must be able to explain what he or she does and why, so that the meaning of what everyone does is clear to themselves and to others. Each individual must be able to answer the "So what?" questions until their activities are not just explained logically but connected to their hearts. Doing this is like integrating and activating the nerve system. It is like having a good foothold while engaging in battle. In sailing, this is like scrubbing the deck, galley, or bulkhead while keeping an eye out for weather and hazards ahead. In an orchestra, the instrumentalists become one together with their instruments, music scores, ears, eyes, and muscles, devoting all of those elements to the mission at hand—making music.

On one hand is the spiritual quality that should give meaning to whatever we do. On the other hand is the detailed task of "doing the basics." Even though the specifics of the work and our mind may look divided, they are not separate. This again is related to mastering the use of tools. If a mini-company president simply waits for reports from the front line without knowing what is going on, he or she is doomed to fail. The same is true for a salesperson who is concerned only with numbers and does not detect even small changes in his or her client's behavior. Or a machine operator who simply does the assigned task but does not take note of an unusual noise or a drop of oil from the machine.

Mastering the basics hones our intuition and keeps us balanced or centered so that we avoid feeling fragmented or lost in the turbulence. Our brains, hearts, sensory systems, and muscles are well tuned in. The success of each mini-company in a network depends on the other units being focused on the customer-supplier relationship which links them all. This interdependency among mini-companies brings out self-organizing characteristics and helps everyone accomplish the mission. This forms the basis of a healthy operation.

Connecting to the Basic Principle

If we have a warehouse where materials or information is stored temporarily, it is critical that such a place is well organized. If someone asks for an item and it cannot be found because of a lack of organization, unnecessary work has to be initiated—especially when it is an important and urgent item. So good organization is a necessary discipline. This applies not just to the warehouse, but wherever we need to find tools or information quickly. Without such discipline, we will become frustrated searching for specific information or seeking a solution to a problem in our own brains as well. The point here is that a lack of good discipline can lead to chaos and confusion—whether it is at work, or in our own mental processes.

Knowing what to do conceptually is simply not enough. Well-practiced, *good* discipline is the key to accomplishing anything. All sports players, musicians, and professional people go through countless drills and exercises to master their skills. Management is no exception. We need to establish good discipline both organizationally and individually. If we see that the Basics of the Mini-Company provide good discipline, we need to align our minds, attitudes, behaviors, and habits to them. If our mission is really desirable and right, that is what we need to do to find our destiny. Every time we get confused or lost, we need to go through the basics and listen to our heart as many times as it may take to get the point.

These points are to be practiced in the various implementation processes discussed earlier. Then, by internalizing good discipline, our *habits* will change, and therefore our destiny will change. But if we do not ask "So what?" repeatedly, and if the basics of running the mini-company are not exercised, we become like a Samurai warrior who cannot find the sword when he needs it. Just as a disorganized warehouse can cause chaos, if every mini-company is not practicing the basics the whole organization will suffer. We should consider every moment as a new beginning in implementing the basics of the mini-company.

Chapter 7

Mini-Companies in the Dynamics of Today's Business

❖

The ultimate test of our ability to find our destiny operating a company to meet the demands of shareholders, customers, and our surrounding community is whether we can do all that in today's chaotic and dynamic world. Many assumptions are constantly challenged. New technologies including the Internet accelerate the pace of change. At the same time, increased competition requires every company constantly to examine its reason for existence.

Implementing the idea of the mini-company and glass wall management creates a very similar environment *within* the company that stimulates the people's creativity, allowing them to come up with various suggestions and strategies. If we go a step further to the level of individual, we realize that the whole process is similar to what happens in the brain, when new ideas are formulated by breaking down our mental barriers. Just as idea generation may correspond to the reconfiguration of the neuron network, as strategy is implemented, it affects the construct of our society and the individuals within. So, we see interaction happening within and among our society, companies, mini-companies, and individuals, thus creating a very dynamic environment. (See Appendix A for Note on Interconnectedness.)

Relevant information and intelligence should be openly accessible for better use. To do this well, we should free ourselves from having fixed mind-sets so that we can better access this information. We also need to avoid making premature judgments. Running a mini-company and practicing glass wall management can help us harness the creative process.

The Mini-Company and Strategy Development

Strategy may be viewed as a scenario developed by connecting ideas from relevant information sources. Traditionally, strategic planning was done at the top level to determine the future direction of the company. While this may still be the case, the basic goal of strategy is to find a unique way to address the needs of customers. All mini-companies participate in this process through their own business plans. In other words, strategy is the total integration of business plans across the whole organization representing the collected wisdom of the company.

In this process the mini-company's members should first develop their own abilities before exploring opportunities elsewhere on a larger scale. The mini-company environment helps people within to grow and explore their horizon much as companies explore ways to grow within a free enterprise system. Knowing its own business as well as its own strengths and weaknesses, the mini-company can pursue a higher mission if they so desire and with their bankers' support.

A successfully running mini-company will be well organized internally and will have well-established links to customers, suppliers, and bankers. Driven by its vision and mission, and utilizing its resources, it will openly search for opportunities. This is a creative process tied to its mission. In this way, formulating strategy or a business plan is a search for the best combination of 5W1H—who is to do what, when, where, why, and how. Doing this in concert with other mini-companies and their members is similar to playing catch with various parties. It is a form of brainstorming.

To develop a strategy in such an environment, the mini-company should be open, inquisitive, and entrepreneurial. Formulating a new strategy represents a new neuron linkage in our brain or a unique combination of memories and logic that results in a new insight. In an organization, such a new linkage is manifested as a new business configuration. Mergers, acquisitions, partnerships, or restructuring may be components of the company strategy as a part of the continuous reconstruction of business. Similarly, the mini-company on its own initiative should also search for a strategy that makes sense to its members in its own universe.

The Mini-Company Is the Strategy

Implementing mini-company ideas is a strategy in itself. Here is the essence of why practicing the mini-company is the strategy, and what makes it a successful strategy:

- The company's success depends upon the potential of its people.
- To tap this potential, the company reaches out to each individual.
- Individuals search the core of their being to find meaning in what they do by asking "So what?" repeatedly.
- Bankers or the mini-company president will provide guidance as needed.
- The initiative of the people should be tied to situational leadership, i.e., find something at work that they believe in, that they like, and that they can be proud of.
- People's creativity is fostered through the self-organizing process by such means as bankers' meetings, the glass wall, and open day.

- The mini-company brings out the entrepreneurial spirit of people while developing general management skills to run the mini-company.
- The mini-company encourages autonomous management. There is no other way but to practice this as the business becomes more fluid and complex.
- Evaluation is still done in a businesslike manner by bankers. Rigorous analytical ability is needed. Here, checks and balances on the glass wall help the learning process.
- The mini-company encourages people to find their own destiny.
- To bring out people's potential, managers need to understand the universe their people live in and be able to speak their language.

As mentioned before, the terms "we" and "they" are interchangeable. As much as we are a part of the whole, we also represent the whole of what we manage. Being aware of this may help us to figure out the strategy that makes sense for all, and at the same time avoid being self-centered. If we can relate to and be able to identify with others, then a stronger team spirit will develop. Benefits which come from flexibility and the self-organizing process depend on acquiring this basic viewpoint.

The Strategy Development Process

The strategy for a mini-company may be called its business plan. Typically, such plans are formalized every six months or yearly, as a part of the plan for the whole company. They should fit into the framework shown in exhibit 4.1. The process of coordination involves matching up the plans and available resources. The bankers' meeting is the platform to accomplish this.

As discussed in chapter 3, problems or opportunities should be identified first. To do this, each mini-company collects information from its customers, suppliers, bankers, and its members. Glass wall management facilitates this process. As mentioned, it is like playing soccer. We should know where the ball is at all times.

To be used effectively, the glass wall should help us to reflect on what is important or urgent, and what we are going to do about it. Posting misleading, outdated, or unorganized information defeats this purpose. Although we must prevent the leakage of information to competitors, the potential of the glass wall to unleash the creative power of the total organization outweighs the potential negatives by a wide margin. Making the whole company's business process transparent is an important part of this strategy. In summary, in order to collect intelligence wisely and eliminate biased opinion, everyone should review and follow the Basics of the Mini-Company (chapter 2) and practice the principles of glass wall management.

Key Factors in Developing a Sound Strategy

The focus in this book has been on the process more than the specific contents. This is based on the idea that a sound process brings about sound results. Since specific strategies or business plans will vary widely among mini-companies, we cannot go into great detail here. We will however look into key factors that can influence the mini-company's strategy. They are:

- *Mental attitude:* Strategy is not sound if managerial leadership is missing and people do not share a vision. For example, even though some people may want to gain more responsibility because they think that it equates to personal success, be warned that increasing the size of the mini-company could be a mistake. We should make such decisions with a cool head.

- *Consistency of strategy:* The cumulative impact of specific plans and overall strategy has to be consistent not only at the mini-company but also at the corporate level. In order to respond to a dynamic, changing environment, being somewhat inconsistent may not necessarily be bad. Yet the mini-company president and the bankers must keep their eyes on the most critical areas and prepare attractive alternatives that can be executed without delay.

- *Link with the business environment:* An important purpose of a viable strategy is to ensure the long-run success of the organization. Since the business environment is constantly changing, managers need to assess the degree to which plans developed are consistent with the environment as it exists now. It is like aiming at a moving target. We have to be concerned with the current position as well as the speed and direction of movement. The failure to do this can be costly.

- *Link with critical resources:* As a mini-company tries to respond to threats and opportunities perceived in its business, it should evaluate items like core competence, people's talents, budgetary constraints, and physical setup to know where its strengths *and* weaknesses lie. Then the mini-company needs to match the strengths to its opportunities and protect the weaknesses from threats. The potential energy of the organization needs to be channeled to focus on key issues.

- *Achieving a balance:* One of the most difficult issues in setting strategy is achieving a balance between strategic objectives and available resources. This requires a careful estimate of resources to achieve particular objectives in a timely manner. The most common mistakes result from failing to make these estimates or being too optimistic about them. Going through the PDCA cycle helps people learn this skill in an empirical manner.

- *Assessment of risks:* What appears to be a sound idea may also be risky. More resources, long-term projects, and a higher proportion of resources committed to a single venture typically constitute a higher risk. Consequently, each mini-company and its bankers need to decide how much risk they want to live with. For this purpose, probabilities of various scenarios need to be evaluated. Alternatives such as licensing or joint ventures should be considered to broaden the resource base. However, we should remember that the best strategy is not necessarily the one with the lowest risk.

- *Making the strategy workable:* To create a workable strategy, here are a few more suggestions: (a) develop efficient and effective communication and coordination processes; (b) seek a consensus about strategy development, execution, and follow-up; (c) maintain consistent policies such as a personnel appraisal system that matches the strategic focus; and (d) recruit or develop talent to provide management with the time and the room to maneuver.

Business Development by Mini-Companies

Well-run mini-companies can produce miracles! They represent a powerful form of the value creation process. Tremendous improvement in performance of quality, cost, delivery, safety, and morale is seen across the board. Furthermore, the initiatives of a mini-company can create a new approach to business and possibly a new organization. Whether such an organization remains within the company, a joint task force, or newly established entity is a matter to be decided. Organization follows the need—not the other way around. To illustrate this, here are few examples of business development by mini-companies.

George, the manager of a shipping department in a 350-employee manufacturer in South Carolina, runs the department with twenty trucks delivering the finished products nationwide. After careful study of the costs and benefits, George proposed to his bankers that the trucks be used to deliver products for other companies as well. Even though this required more detailed tracking of the trucks and careful contractual negotiations, the mini-company president and his people succeeded in convincing the bankers of the viability of their business plan. Now more than one-third of the company's profit comes from this mini-company.

Facing the need to increase production by 20 percent to meet a sudden increase in demand on top of what was predicted for the Christmas season, Hans, the CEO of a 2,500-employee company in Germany, asked all employees of the company to work extra overtime. Before mini-company ideas were implemented, top management would have thought it impossible for employees to respond to such a request. As it turned out, virtually all employees agreed to the request without hesitation.

In a 150-employee company in California, Gustavo, a young immigrant employee, proposed improvements to his mini-company president. His four-page proposal, which included drawing new layouts and detailed cost calculations, resulted in four fewer employees needed to do the job in this fifteen-employee department. Managers were quite embarrassed that the idea had not come from them. Still, everybody was very happy and nobody lost their job as a result. Meanwhile, the company continued to grow successfully over the years that followed.

There are numerous ways a mini-company can apply its creativity in business development. For example, it can sell excess capacity, create new business with core competences, form licensing arrangements, develop partnerships for new product development, acquire or hire capable individuals, sell competitors' products, vertically integrate, and on and on. Our imagination is the limit. Mini-companies can initiate strategy formation on their own with their bankers' approval. If the bankers do not approve, the people in the mini-company may even consider leaving the company to pursue their dream.

Does this sound too radical? Do we have enough faith to cultivate such a culture? How much autonomy can be given to mini-companies to explore their potential? Can all bankers guide a mini-company properly? For the organization to move forward, those questions need to be answered. The premise of the mini-company idea is based on the dynamics of people pursuing a dream and accomplishing something meaningful for society.

The mini-company should propose its business plans just as any startup company would do to the venture capitalists. The annual report should indicate its track record and management capability. Naturally, these documents should be carefully prepared and well organized to communicate what this mini-company is all about. Unlike situations where people are left in the dark without much choice but to work like slaves following decisions that have been made elsewhere, the mini-company will provide an environment for people to actively seek out their future, which, at the same time, can improve the prospects of the company.

Creating a Supportive Environment

Our work environment should help identify needs and interests in people. If Newton were not interested in scientific discovery, no matter how many times he saw apples dropping from the tree, he would not have discovered the law of gravity. In our case, we identify needs from the glass wall and by questioning "So what?" to focus our energy on the critical issues.

Inspiration comes when there is no artificial force applied while sufficient information is provided as a resource to respond to a need. To facilitate inspiration, people from various backgrounds should meet in an informal setting every now and then. Again, the "kindergarten effect" suggests associating playfulness and openness with such an environment. The mini-company open day is an occasion to share the concerns and progress of mini-company activities. Presentations and exhibitions help to stimulate the exchange of ideas and fresh viewpoints in a fun environment. The open day can be virtually a big brainstorming session where everybody can teach or learn lessons while networking among people with similar concerns. Knowledge, problem consciousness, fun, and networking are all important ingredients to formulate sound strategy. As a dynamic business environment is developed by dynamic individuals, we certainly need to create such an opportunity to foster the strategy development process.

A case in point: In a large multinational company, top management decided to restructure the company with a strategic business unit approach. Even though this made sense, cross-fertilizing of ideas across business units became difficult. So, they continued to schedule meetings where management could share the progress of mini-companies from around the world, providing an important learning and morale boosting opportunity. Many think that ongoing education helps top management to stay on the cutting edge of the learning, but what about the rest of the organization? What about learning from within? Who has the initiative, insight, and ingenuity to discover this hidden treasure? Remember, one of the mini-company principles is: "Whoever feels the pain should take action."

Creating a Core Competence and Bringing Out the Meaning

One way to develop strategy is to see how value chains can be broken up and reconfigured to provide a more value-added service to the customers. As boundaries are taken away and assumptions challenged, business will try to find the best combination of the key factors of 5W1H, or, people, management, financial resources, time, location, technology, suppliers, and customers. Accordingly, various business models are proposed and restructuring of companies and industries takes place continuously. In other words, this is a total resource allocation process to make the most of what we have.

The process is like solving a jigsaw puzzle. However, the difference here is that each piece of that puzzle—that is, the company or mini-company—is constantly trying to renew itself on its own by redefining the reasons for its existence in order to better meet the needs of customers. In other words, the mini-company should take initiative to (a) develop its core competency in what it does, and (b) match that capability with the needs of business to add maximum value. Here the core competency to match the needs of business should be shown clearly, for example, in the mini-company annual report. The annual report should stress key messages like:

"This is what we are about. This is our vision. We are proud of what we do. This is how we manage. Here is the evidence of what we have collectively accomplished."

After this, we still need to keep exploring in order to fine tune capabilities according to the changing needs of the business. Here, the glass wall should help because of the ease of access to key information. Then we should find that the whole process is reciprocal. That is, as more mini-companies produce annual reports and utilize the glass wall, the exploration process will be much easier for all to go through. The reverse is also true: If the mini-company cannot use the annual report or glass wall to explain what they do, what is important, why, and what are the main problems, that narrows the avenues left available to access the intelligence of others.

The harder we try to find ways to satisfy the needs of customers or society and try to find our own destiny, the more we realize that we cannot be self-centered. We need to listen carefully and appreciate the links to others in order to sustain or build up our core competence. As we reflect on changes in our industry and in our customers' needs, we realize that our competence itself needs to change to meet those needs. To rephrase this, we are nobody without everybody. Whether it is the skills we acquire, the products we use, the food we eat, or even the genes we inherit, they represent a part of the customer-supplier relationship. We need to have a real appreciation of what we can do in business and in our life, having been given the opportunity to play the game.

How Mini-Companies Interact with Other Business Units

Mini-companies interact with different parties in a variety of ways to explore new ideas that may yield practical implications for business development.

Competing with Other Mini-Companies in the Same Company

Here bankers perform the function of referees. Healthy competition brings out innovative ideas. Monopolies and rigid structures should be challenged. The notion of cooperation for the total good is counterbalanced by the notion of competition. Examples include different teams competing to develop new products or processes, different factories competing to produce products in different locations, and different mini-companies competing to get necessary resources from the bankers.

Competing with Other Mini-Companies from outside the Company

Because of the rapid pace of change in business and technology, any function of a mini-company can be disrupted or eliminated all of a sudden. Instead of waiting for this to happen, the mini-company should gather information to expose potential threats or opportunities. They should also benchmark competitors to improve their own unique capabilities. Potential threats may include contract or temporary services like engineering, research and development, sales, accounting, bookkeeping, consultants, and various technological advancements.

Cooperating with Other Mini-Companies from outside the Company

When internal resources are limited or the necessary competence is lacking, a mini-company can cooperate with other mini-companies that have expertise in some particular area such as sales, engineering, or research and development. However, if this core competency is not sustainable, cooperation may result in an erosion of the business.

Dealing with Other Mini-Companies outside the Company

To deliver the best possible product or service to the customer, companies are constantly searching for ways to create the best value chain. Here, the focus is on its competence. The constant structural change taking place through mergers and acquisitions, supply chain management, and reengineering efforts reflects this issue of redefining the value chain to provide the most value-added for society. This is certainly good for customers. Products they buy can come from parts made in India, China, or Brazil. The bottom line is the best performance in quality, cost, and delivery. So, with approval from higher management, any mini-company can become a buyer or supplier of products or services even if the business partner is a competitor. This is happening in many industries, espcially in the consumer appliance and electronic industries.

Selling and Buying Mini-Companies

A company may sell or buy mini-companies in the process of redefining its strategy. The mini-company then has to find its destiny with new owners, and possibly new suppliers or customers. What then is the future of the mini-company and its people? Ultimately, it is the new owner of the mini-company who will determine the future. If the mini-company has demonstrated a good track record in its annual report, it is likely that the new owner will let the mini-company manage itself.

Mini-companies usually help new owners and bankers assess their capability accurately. What better way to judge than to have people of the mini-company explain their capabilities and mission? I have encountered several cases in which the whole company was sold at a premium price because of their well-run mini-company operations. As management practice speaks for itself, the transition to a new environment is usually very smooth. The new owners often try to incorporate the mini-company idea in their own organization.

Restructuring of Mini-Companies

Whether internal to the company or not, restructuring may be done at the initiative of the mini-company supported by its bankers. Generally it is easy for mini-company people to fit into a new environment. Applying the acquired skill to organized management information, problems are exposed quickly allowing everyone to respond.

I have seen mini-companies "merged and acquired" within the company at their own initiative. As much as needs are felt at where the action is, people are much more receptive to go through the necessary structural changes. Clearly displayed facts on the glass wall make restructuring easier by limiting biased opinions. For this same reason, the placement or replacement of personnel, for example through promotion or demotion, is usually much better received in the mini-company environment.

Finding a New Career

If your boss is not utilizing your talents, should you take the initiative to find your own destiny elsewhere—to find a new banker even outside the company? Here, your annual report should speak for itself. If you seek a new banker, the report should serve as a good resume to prove how you managed your mini-company in the past. Having gone through many bankers' meetings to prove your reason for existence, you should have learned to present your case succinctly to potential bankers.

In practice, however, I have seen but a very few cases where such a career move happened. It may be that if a company practices the mini-company idea, it creates a positive environment and appreciates people's talents. For example, when a Spanish company won a European quality prize for practicing mini-company management, they founded a consulting company with its managers to benefit the nation's industries. Gradually building up its capabilities to serve the customers, it is bringing promising results.

The mini-company annual report is sometimes used to supplement the yearly performance appraisal. The report may be somewhat "free form" to encourage people's creativity, and perhaps because of that, the report highlights points that are difficult to convey by the more formal appraisal process.

Key Factors in Running a Mini-Company Successfully

The list below summarizes the key factors for successfully running a mini-company. You may add or delete items from the list, however, or make your own list. Remember, don't take my word for it. Always trust your heart.

- Have a mission. Have a dream. Have the initiative to go for it.
- Don't get hung up. Worry, anger, hate, and suffering are misuses of our imagination. Let us carefully monitor the wrong use of our brain.
- Challenge the fixed mind-set. Challenge the status quo.
- The solution is found in the brain and the heart.
- Start small, introduce a heartbeat, gain momentum, share your progress, and celebrate the efforts with your colleagues.
- Be practical. Encourage trials. Promote creative ideas.
- Examine your actions by asking "So what?" repeatedly.
- Realize that all of us can contribute something. The mini-company can make this happen.

- Promote friendship to share ideas and develop a network.
- Think of work as a game. Create an open atmosphere.
- Be honest with yourself and express what you feel from the heart.
- Realize that each of us is master of his or her own destiny.
- What our heart desires that is right by the laws of nature is not impossible.
- Accept fate and those things beyond your control.
- Never lose hope. Find the meaning in what you do. Have fun in the process.

Key Message
- Use your brain. Listen to your heart. Live with the mission.

Chapter 8

Finding Our Destiny

❖

Mastering our tools is one thing. Mastering ourselves is quite another. I cannot overemphasize that we must understand what is *in our mind* before we can progress to the next step. We must keep asking the "So what?" questions until we can go no further. Especially when we begin to think of ourselves as professionals we must think with the beginner's mind to master our destiny. However, when we find answers to our questions too easily, our life may not be as much fun or as meaningful. The challenge is to be able to sort out distracting noise and delusions and find the best solutions we can. We may try to find a quiet place where the noise doesn't disturb us, or we may have to find a way to move on in spite of the noise around us.

While the future is unknown all living species have unknown potential to explore the undefined world as well. We must reach out for the distant star while living the best we can at *each moment*. As an individual or as a company, the setting is the same. So, in this last chapter, let us see if we can tie this mini-company idea with the core of our existence to prepare us for the journey ahead.

Survival of the Fittest

As any living being does, our business follows the laws of nature. One of the basic principles here is "survival of the fittest." We are fortunate that democracy, the free enterprise system, and an open society give us the opportunity to search for various ways to express ourselves. Interacting with others who will help us surmount the barriers provides the opportunity to create something of higher meaning.

While all of current existence may be seen as the outcome of all past challenges and struggles, in the case of business, proof of our existence is ultimately shown in its bottom line, that is, profit. Profit represents how the company is received by its customers and, in fact, by society as a whole. Just like obtaining food to sustain life, the money earned is then utilized for further growth in the future. This is true for mini-companies as well.

If the mini-company can prove its existence through its quarterly or annual report, and its business plans can convince its bankers to let it continue operating, it should be on its way to accomplishing its mission. Of course, one mini-company cannot by itself move on without establishing links with other mini-companies. So, a broader understanding of business is required to keep addressing its needs and finding the passage to move on—*continuously*. From the bankers' viewpoint, one way to assess the mini-company is to break up the company's operation into many mini-companies to see if any of the operations can be replaced or even eliminated by new technologies. From the bankers' standpoint, whether the mini-company continues to exist within the company may not be an issue because the major concern is the financial health of the larger company and the survival of the bankers.

We have increasing numbers of mergers and acquisitions as industries are modernized. Just as people move on to better opportunities, companies and mini-companies are constantly reconfiguring themselves so that more value-added is provided with fewer resources. It appears that there is no way to stop this process. To better allocate resources, new management principles are also introduced. These changes can be painful. On the other hand, we must acknowledge that the process exposes waste and often results in better ways to serve customers. So, while we are confronted with the cold reality of the survival of the fittest, we can also see that better use of talents and resources in the long run will benefit customers and society. These dynamics cannot be separated.

Finding Meaning

In the discussion above, profitability was emphasized as an important measure of the reason for existence. Sometimes each person's financial contribution to the company is measured individually to demonstrate his or her reason for existence. However, look at the other side of the coin. What if the company is profitable but people are not happy at work? What is the point of such an operation? Shouldn't running a mini-company be an integral part of our *life's* journey?

If we say the mini-company president is the master of his area of responsibility, are we not asking if his heart is in it? When the mini-company annual report is published, are we not asking if the pride in work is in it? Words like heart or pride may still sound simplistic or sentimental to some. But if heart and pride do not count, we may end up becoming slaves of business or money and lose our perspective on life. Or we may be able to prove the reason for existence for someone else, but not be truthful or honest with ourselves.

Just as companies and mini-companies need to explore ways to find and justify the reason for their existence, each of us must *ask* ourselves the questions again and again, and listen to our hearts carefully as we move on in our journey.

Wendy, a manager I met in Wisconsin, once told me that

she practices the mini-company idea at home. She orchestrates various activities for her family, gathers ideas from family members, and prioritizes plans. Naturally I was happy to hear this. Readers who are interested in learning how mini-company ideas are tied to our life's process should see Appendix B, Beyond the Mini-Company: Life Management.

The Importance of Asking Questions

To keep ourselves engaged, we need to keep asking questions. In fact, we even need to ask ourselves what the right questions are. If that requires deliberate effort, patience, time, and energy, so be it. In my opinion it is much better to find the right problem to work on than to continue to keep solving the wrong problems indefinitely. I believe the questions we ask ourselves define the perimeter of our thinking, attitude, behavior, habit—and our *destiny*. "As a man thinks in his heart, so is he."

We need to continue to ask questions even when it seems that no answers are in sight. Even if we do not have an answer immediately, asking the right question will eventually lead us to land on the right problem to work on. It is a test to see if we are connecting our thinking and behavior to a principle of business practice—and, of course, *our life*. If what we consider urgent issues distract us in the short term or if emotional winds disturb our vision, the basics still have to be taken care of.

Here are few of the questions we can ask ourselves every now and then:

- What do you think is going on?
- What is important? What is your main concern?
- Why?

- What is the point?
- If it is important, can you prove or show me that it is so?
- If you cannot, does that mean it is unclear in your mind? If so, what will you do?
- How can I see what you say you are doing is actually happening?
- Where is the proof?
- Is there anything I can do for you? ("I" here may represent our own consciousness, or the source of our wisdom. In other words, are you ready to listen?)
- So what? (Show me the reason of existence. Speak with your own words, directly coming from your heart.)

These questions may sound rough or blunt. We may just skim through them without trying to answer from the depth of our being. We may ask questions just as we habitually do any task—like a robot—or we may become slaves of our own mental conditioning. But with sincere efforts and repeated practice, such questioning *will* eventually bring an awareness of our being into a clearer light. We may realize that our habitually fixed mind-set or conditioned response is the source of delusions. But I hope that because we want to clear up these issues, we will ask questions. The more serious and difficult the dilemma is, the more diligently we need to work on it. Our problem may be related to external events or internal matters in our mind. We may undertake this questioning on our own or with others. If we practice this with our banker or mini-company president, and the point becomes clear to the person whom we are questioning, we will all smile and go on with life because we know we are touching the essence. If our direction is still unclear or unresolved even after questioning or guidance, then we will still smile and go on with life because that may be all we can do for the time being.

I have conducted many seminars on mini-companies. When I get a question, I often ask, "What do you think?" or even "Why do you ask that question?" In most cases, questioners can find the solution by themselves. By trying out an idea they will learn the lesson, then make corrections as needed. Here, the fundamental point of my own questioning is to get the questioner back to his home—the starting point—to enable the questioner to begin again. Meister Eckhart said, "Be willing to be a beginner every single morning," and that is the point. Especially when we are lost, we need to do this. Of course the possibility exists that we do not know that we are lost. In such a case, our earnest questioning should lead to such a realization.

The Solution Is within Us

To find solutions we need to do our homework. The more homework we do, the better equipped we will become. Questioning ourselves sincerely without accepting any shallow answers, and then re-questioning ourselves is the best training we can have to develop self-managing capability. The specifics of this questioning process may be different for each person. Then, a key to mastering our destiny is the conviction gained from the experience of finding our own solutions.

The process is like playing catch with our conscience. We have to do this continuously, reaching to the core of our being, to come up with the solution that is most genuine. Our minds may be compared to a glass wall, imprinted with all our experiences, that will organize itself to provide the solution. Being the master is realizing when we are lost and being able to get back home. Being the master is coming up with the solution. Being the master is using our creativity to find a solution that others also appreciate. We are being tested and testing ourselves all the time.

Some people have already taken this test. Listen to the words of the Zen master Dogen (also see Appendix C, Listening to the Masters):

"To know the way is to learn about ourselves.
To learn about ourselves is to forget ourselves.
To forget ourselves is to be proven by the laws of the uni-
verse.
To be proven by the laws of universe is to awaken the
mind/body of our own and of others."

This passage contains the essence of learning by asking questions—by devoting ourselves to accomplishing the mission to the point of forgetting ourselves. When we find the moment of oneness or inspiration—the moment when we are convinced of the meaning of our being—it is like touching a live wire. Whatever the subject is, at that instant all potential is expressed fully and we become the master.

Most—probably all—of us wish to experience *true* prosperity, peace, and happiness. Yet realizing that dream may seem impossible for some. While there are other reasons for this, the fundamental reason can be traced to how we perceive ourselves. The use we make of our minds and our attitudes and habits may not reflect the law of nature. We may look south to search for the North Star, or we may try to bend the elbow outward to gain freedom, thinking that our way is correct. To realize our dreams, we must develop our minds, attitudes, behavior, and habits to follow nature's way.

After attending my seminar on the mini-company, Eva, a senior executive of a large multinational company, asked me a question. She told me later that I responded by saying "If you keep asking that question of yourself, and if you really want to get the answer, eventually you will find the answer." When we met again several months later, she told me that she had been confused by my response at the time. But later she found that what I said then was quite true, and she thanked me for letting her find her own answer.

We may give "textbook" answers at times. But, if we are really concerned about developing people to become masters of their destiny, *not* giving the straight answer may be the best thing we can do. The most useful answers are those found inside of us based on what we have learned from our life experiences.

In summary:

- Asking questions forces us to be truthful, sincere, honest, and clear about why we exist and what mission we have, and makes us base our actions accordingly.
- By questioning ourselves continuously, we will come up with solutions.
- Live accordingly. Have time to reflect.
- If we feel vulnerable, we should remind ourselves that this process is the right one.
- The solution can always be found within us.

About Mastery

We may come to realize that we are the solution. This is because *we* represent the summation of all that has happened in the past. Words, thoughts, medicine, discoveries, and inventions that help our life are all gifts from the past. We may even realize that our *life* itself is a gift. We must use these gifts to contribute what we can, and pass our work on to others or to the next generation. In that sense, no person who lived in the past is gone. Their efforts and lives are reflected in our actions and what we see around us.

We owe it to those who lived in the past to be happy with

what we have but to continue the journey to pursue our dreams. I believe that is their will, just as it is our obligation to the people of the future to leave the seeds and the outcome of our work for them to build their lives upon. Even though we may be engrossed in our daily lives, we should not forget the roots from which we came and the reasons why we are here.

Whether we are feeling successful or unsuccessful, we should ask where we got our ideas about success and failure. Mission accomplished, made money, still unhappy. This is not the state of mind we should seek. To be master of our destiny is to be aware of false values and delusions. Confusion or struggle exists when there is something "separate" in us. When our brains alone control our lives, we may sense despair. But if we live from the heart, we can achieve the absolute state of being.

The heart is the master. Life can be lived from the heart, and connected to the brain when necessary. Then, freedom is realized when the heart quietly observes the struggle in the brain and provides its own answer, following nature's way. So, we make our own living as best as we can. We cannot totally control what happens to us. However, we *can* control how we feel or how we respond to what we feel. I believe the essence of life is found in this unknown potentiality. Only in our heart, we find the foundation of us living as genuine human beings, mastering our own destiny.

In our life's journey, earthly desires may still show up continuously. Or, our mechanical minds may try to take over or get us stuck in a cul-de-sac. Again and again, this is when we need to *recognize* the confused state of our mind and patiently and calmly *observe* what is going on. Then we need to *listen* carefully to the message coming from the heart. We should ask if we are on the right course. Patiently wait for the insight, and take the next step to continue our journey. In other words, we should use our brains, listen to our hearts, and live with our mission. (See Appendix D for the Characteristics of the Masters.)

Is this is not what mastery, success, and happiness are all about? If it is the case, can we be truly the masters of the mini-companies? Wherever we are and whatever our past, we can paint on the canvas of our universe the total existence of our life and see how it may unfold. And, in this journey of our life, may we hear our heart continue to whisper, "When we give up, that is when we fail. If we do not give up, there is no failure."

"As he thinks in his heart, so is he."
(Proverbs 25:7)

Epilogue

✦

"So What?"

We have tried to establish that the meaning of all we search for is ultimately to be found in the hearts that we are born with. Asking questions repeatedly and conscientiously is the centerpiece of pursuing our life's mission. Everything we do has a connection to that very point. The mini-company is the way to achieve our goal at work. The same principle applies to our life management.

Our minds, attitude, behavior, and habits should reflect this principle. We need to work on this principle to become one with our mission. This involves overcoming noises, disruptions, and the whispering of devils that cloud the picture. My colleague Fred once said, "It was like being hit by a stick at the exact moment when my bad habits were about to take over." We all need a good mental "stick" in our personal lives to remind us to correct our bad habits and keep us on track.

If we reflect back to moments of inspiration or compassion that we have experienced, we may find that these moments arose from the same source—our hearts. Just as the masters diligently expressed what was in their hearts, I am certain that each of us can do likewise.

The important thing is to *do*. Utilize what is given to us. Do the best we can. Inevitably we will experience delusions and distractions because our minds have been programmed by the past, but that is also why we can be awakened. For example, we may feel envious of those who have certain qualities or have accomplished a lot. The mass media promote such envy. But, if we are not careful, such stimuli will make us slaves of our earthly desires. So, again, listen to your heart.

When he was an apprentice, Mr. Matsushita used to take a bath after a day's hard work. Reflecting on the work he had done that day, he felt grateful to have that bath. As small an incident as it may be, I sense that there is mastery at work—fully utilizing what he had and focusing on the task at hand. And even many years later, he may have felt the same humble gratitude when the company he founded, then known as Matsushita Electric, broke a ten billion dollar sales record. I sense that such is the beginner's mind that is always new and *alive*.

A Bird in a Cage

At the end of a seminar in Taiwan a few years ago, a participant came up to the podium and drew a picture of a bird in a cage on an overhead slide. The door of this cage was open and a sign on the cage read "Mini-Company." After telling me that he liked my seminar he went on to say that he felt like that caged bird as he listened to me talk about the vision of the mini-company.

He said that he wanted to fly out and explore. The door was open. But he wasn't sure if he should. Finally he asked me, "What should I do?" I paused and asked him, "What do you think?" The mini-company is a new way of looking at work and life, I said. Not being told what to do, not being a slave of anything. Each one of us needs to find our way to be the master of what we do. So, good luck!

After I concluded a seminar in the Philippines by sharing

this episode of the bird in a cage I went out to lunch with the group. The first dish we had was a roasted pigeon! Seeing this, we all laughed, saying, "Hope we won't end up like this if we fly out of the cage." Yet there are questions still remaining. Is it worth the effort to fly out if there is danger out there? What is our choice? I cannot tell you what to do. It is for each of us to figure out, doing the best we can and listening to our heart. In this process, I hope we do not lose hope, initiative, and the energy to explore the world and find meaning in it. Otherwise, we may conduct our lives carrying a cage around us that exists only in our imagination.

Green—The Color of Hope

In nature, green represents the ever-renewing energy of trees and grass. Year after year, through cold winters, dry summers, or violent storms, trees never give up. They grow to explore and rise to the heavens. If we listen to them, they may speak to us in the way they practice their "mini-companies," utilizing all they have, never complaining, and never stopping their journey.

In my own journey, I have traveled millions of miles to conduct seminars for thousands of managers, visited hundreds of companies, and met many thousands of people. Once I asked a factory operator in Indonesia, "Is it too demanding to practice this mini-company idea?" The employee said, "No, not at all. It is an opportunity for me to grow." Yvonne, a mini-company president at a Dutch company, told me how top management was so excited when they read her mini-company's first annual report that they launched mini-companies in hundreds of their plants throughout the world. I cannot describe how moved I was to hear these voices.

In the Introduction the question was posed: "How shall we find our destiny and what are the principles with which we can identify?" As you have discovered, the specific answer will vary. But we know that all answers are connected to the core of our existence where never-ending hope is being created. It is my hope that the seeds sown here will grow and continue to produce flowers and more seeds. At the same time, I also hope that we will do our best on our journey and find our own destiny both in business and in life, and that we will keep green, the color of hope, foremost in our mind.

"It Is OK"

Most of us have experienced suffering in our lives, and some of us have caused suffering in others. When we go through such experiences, we may be preoccupied and unaware of what our hearts are attempting to tell us. Yet listening to its "voice" and becoming aware of what is really happening is essential if we are to live truly fulfilled lives.

Even though we are ultimately one with that voice, illusions get in the way. To deal with them, we must discipline ourselves to listen. The voice may be heard in different ways. It may come to us as compassion, as wisdom, as an inspiring message, or as a clearer understanding of our true nature.

Walking the hiking trail by myself one day, I thought about this and said to myself, "I am sorry that I did not listen to you." As I saw how my mechanical mind had taken over my life, there was no excuse but to see that I had caused pain and suffering for me as well as for others. So, I was playing catch with my heart reflecting on some instances in my life. Though I had not intended to cause suffering to others, or to myself, I had ended up doing so. With that realization, tears started to run. I wished that I had listened, and had prevented anyone from suffering. Then, I heard a voice saying, "It is OK." It came from deep inside my heart. More tears flowed. I felt that they came from the same source as the tears of others who have gone through the same experience. I felt totally forgiven.

As my journey continues, I have no clue about what is waiting. "It is OK" was an answer to my "So what?" question. I will keep asking "So what?" on my journey—perhaps to confirm that it is OK again and again. If so, it is OK. If it is not so, ultimately, it is OK as well. This book is an answer to that question. The words written here may be soon dead just like the song of a bird. But even so, they were once alive, the best I had at that time. And that is OK.

When we give up, that is when we fail. If we do not give up, there is no failure in life. If we are truthful to our hearts, and live according to the truth, we find our destiny. Or, we may realize that we ourselves are our destiny. So, good luck in your journey. Even if it is a difficult one, remember to listen to the heart and spare some time to find little flowers blooming by the roadside—as much as we are one of them after all.

From the Heart—The Principle Way

In this book, perhaps one of the first in management books, I attempted to straightforwardly address the subject of, "Use your brain. Listen to your heart. And, live with the mission." We have seen many books on management theory that focus mainly on how we use the brain to manage, but often miss the point of connecting to the heart. On the other hand, we have also seen many books on motivation, leadership, and organizational learning process, but that often lack the link to the logical construct of management. Often, the results are the dichotomy and the gap created in between.

So, I have attempted to illustrate how our brain part of

management practice is connected to our heart. It is as if the means have been found to connect to our genuine initiative. Then, to put this idea into practice, I introduced a comprehensive and pragmatic principle called the "mini-company." Practicing this idea should also help to identify the individual's pursuit of his life's journey tied to the organization needs. When this total picture is captured and our efforts put into practice, we should find how our "Life Energy" is channeled productively, contributing to the progress of our society. Realizing this is the aim of this book—*Results from the Heart.*

What is also interesting here is that this mini-company idea is tied to a web-like flexible structure of the organization where every one is a part of the whole but at the same time, a whole of what he manages. This is called a "Holon" structure where *holos* (whole) and *on* (individual) find a harmony as in any biological or social organizations. Not only is this similar to what is happening in the World Wide Web, but this also represents our brain's neuron structure where memories are stored in a holographic manner as a source of intelligence—to create something new and meaningful. So, from neuron to individual to mini-company to company to society, we find the function of a self-initiated living entity—that is, the mini-company—channeling its energy and utilizing linkage mechanism for the expression of life for all. Then, when we gain this as direct experience as it is expressed everywhere, however limited we may feel about ourselves at times, it may be like touching a live wire, or finding the principle way of the universe and *living* it.

Appendix A

A Note on Interconnectedness

❖

Interconnected characteristics found among our society, companies, mini-companies, and to the level of individuals' neurons have an interesting similarity to the Kegon philosophy of
Buddhism, Arthur Koestler's Holon paradigm, and the quantum interconnectedness of Bohm, Bohr, and Heisenberg as
briefly explained below:

1. In Kegon philosophy, it is called the mystery of principal and satellites. This means that every element in a
   conditional nexus can be looked upon as a hub, or
   "principal," whereupon all the other elements become
   the cooperative conditions, or "satellites" to all the
   other elements. It is the mutuality, the complementar-
   ity, of the elements which makes them functionally
   what they are (p. 44, Thomas Cleary, *Shobogenzo*,
   University of Hawaii Press, 1986). The Buddhavatam-
   saka (Kegon)-sutra emphasizes mutually unobstructed
   interpenetration, called Jijimuge in Japanese, as witnessed in our life and any form of organization where
   the whole and the individuals foster one another.

2. Arthur Koestler coined a word, Holon as a combination
   of *holos* (whole) + *on* (individual). It brings a holistic
   view of living organisms and social organizations with
   "an identifiable part of a system that has a unique identity, yet is made up of subordinate parts and, in turn, is
   part of a larger whole" (*The Ghost in the Machine*, 1969;

JANUS 1978). Other characteristics of Holon may include self-organizing, synchronizing, coexisting of autonomous and complementing nature, entraining, vibrating/fluctuating, and continuously searching for creating new order through creative disruption.

3. Tied to the laws of quantum physics, Bohm brings "an analogy of hologram for the implicate order because of its property that each of its parts, in some sense, contains the whole." Capra also points out: "An indivisible universe, in which all things and events are interrelated, would hardly make sense unless it were self-consistent" (p. 279, 309, *Tao of Physics*, Capra, Bantam Books, 1984). Science has not figured out what consciousness or life energy is. Yet, such experiences as men's awakening and inspiration, the firing mechanism of neurons, as well as the evolution of DNA may be closely related to the unique phenomenon of energy and matter as witnessed in quantum mechanics.

Understanding the interconnectedness of nature should make us realize that each individual cannot exist without depending on others along with infinitely interlinked events. Then, we may find the words of Christ, "Do unto others what you would like them to do to you," represent love and wisdom coming out of the realization of such mutual relatedness. Even though power may transform a person into a robot as we may have witnessed, we may also find that the heart can transform a person into a genuinely living being with an infinite potential of wisdom and compassion. If it is so, the two key questions are: Would we see such transformation originated from our heart infinitely expand to the entire world in accordance with it? Would we actively participate in this process by accomplishing the mission of our mini-company?

While our focus is on management of the mini-company, we may see here a glimpse of what is behind all of our acts—a possible link to what is driving the universe.

Appendix B

Beyond the Mini-Company:
Life Management

❖

Someone once said that within a particle of sand is the whole universe represented. Similarly, in the universe of the mini-company, we find the brain, the heart, people and their lives represented. If we look at our lives as a continuing process of problem solving, we may find that mini-company ideas can be equally applicable to the management of our personal lives. This is where we find the health of the organization is connected to the health of the individual. The following notes may help us understand this concept better and apply it where appropriate.

- *The Mission:* We must have a mission in life if our lives are to mean something. Depending on what is expected of us and what we expect of ourselves, our potential for accomplishment will vary. If our lives involve many endeavors, we may have multiple mini-missions, in such areas as work, family, health, hobbies, and so forth.

- *The Customer-Supplier Relationship:* We need to understand the universe we live in. If our mission is to become a painter, the art-buying public could be our customers, while Picasso or Renoir could serve as the supplier of our inspiration. Whether our mission is financial prosperity, scientific discovery, climbing Mount Everest, or the pursuit of human happiness, we can try to clarify our universe as we play the game of life.

- *Objectives:* The idea that "what gets measured gets done" applies here like marking off the distance on a road map. Practicing positive thinking and image control may be helpful in attempting to imagine as vividly as possible what we finally hope to accomplish. However, we should remember that the most valuable qualities cannot be measured in quantities.

- *Problem Solving:* Practicing the idea of personal glass wall management in our minds may help us tap our accumulated knowledge and experiences from the past. We should concentrate and let the ideas organize themselves. Find a quiet place away from the noise, and let go of unimaginative thoughts, disruptive emotions, and even logic to become one with the problem. Often a problem is like an abscess or a boil that cannot be dealt with until it has healed to the point where it can be treated. Let nature do its job for us.

- *The Business Plan:* When we generate business ideas, they are synthesized as specific plans of action with 5W1H as the basis for implementation. Likewise in our personal planning, we can synthesize ideas into a plan of action to change our behavior or habits. As in business, initiative plays a key role in the success of any such personal plan.

- *The Progress Report:* Writing about personal experiences that have influenced our lives can help us organize our thoughts. Before beginning to write, reflect quietly with a beginner's mind. Then objectively summarize what went right and wrong and why, what lessons you learned, and what you can do about it. If you get in the habit of doing this, you will find that it clears your mind and renews your energy for the passage ahead.

- *Open Day:* We should share our concerns or experiences with others. Not just in person, but also by phone or letters or even on the Internet. Typically, the more clearly organized our thoughts, the more progress we can make. If we cannot find a friend with whom to share ideas, we should continue our efforts on our own rather than join a club of lost people. While it is useful to have the "checks and balances" of other opinions, in the end we have to find our own passage and our path.

- *Developing the Heartbeat:* The PDCA cycle in business provides the heartbeat to get the process going. Likewise in our personal lives, asking "So what?" and listening to our hearts is like playing a game of catch to find the connection between our brain and our heart. Diligently *cultivate* this skill to root out delusions and negative thoughts and remain focused on our mission.

- *Connecting to the Heart:* Our habit of getting stuck in thoughts or caught up in emotion is years old, and that habit may hang on in the most tenacious manner. The only way out is to be equally persistent in cultivating the habit to connect to the heart. When we develop this habit, we will notice when we become stuck in our thought patterns. It is that very noticing which allows us to step out of the problem state and frees us from it, bringing our attention to its proper focus.

Just as frequent use of certain muscles or neurons makes them stronger, we find that repetition is the mother of skill. This is why working on our mind, attitudes, behavior, and habits is important. In other words, it is useless to learn and become knowledgeable if we do not *live* by what we have learned. If we continually renew our intention to fulfill our mission and become one with it by following the laws of nature, we should see amazing things happen in our lives.

Listening to the Masters

❖

Here are some words of wisdom for reference. Even though most of these selections come from outside the business world, they have a connection to the specific contents of this book. They address the essence of human nature. Whether or not we can make these words come alive is up to us. As we read them, therefore, we may reflect on our own situation, and on the contents of this book, and look for the meaning behind these expressions. If we do not get the message readily, it may indicate that our field of vision is still limited. So, let us listen with open minds to discover the destiny of our mini-company and our lives.

"Seek, and you shall find; knock, and it shall be opened to you." (Matt. 7:7)

"What goes out to the world market is not the product. It is the philosophy, the brain of that company." (Soichiro Honda)

"If you want to be a better friend, a richer person, a better parent, a better athlete, a more successful businessman, all you need to do is find models of excellence." (Anthony Robbins)

"What is desirable and right is not impossible." (Henry Ford)

"Man is made great or small by his own will." (Schiller)

"So how can I set myself free?" *"Who has bound you?"*
(Zen Koan)

"I am not discouraged, because every wrong attempt discarded is another step forward." (Thomas Edison)

"When the solution is simple, God is answering."
(Albert Einstein)

"The life which is unexamined is not worth living."
(Plato)

"I did not wish to live what was not life." (Henry David
Thoreau)

"Truth above all, even when it upsets and overwhelms us." (Amiel)

"Youth is youngness at heart. Youth is eternal for those who are full of faith and hope, and greet the challenges of each new day with courage and confidence." (Konosuke Matsushita)

"Those who mistake the unessential to be essential and essential to be unessential, dwelling in wrong thoughts, never arrive at the essential." (Buddha
[Dhammapada II])

"If we do what we have always done, we will get what we have always got." (Found at the wall of a factory floor
in the Midwest)

"Life clears itself to the degree that we understand how the mind works." (Vernon Howard)

"Beware of dissipating your powers; strive constantly to concentrate them." (Goethe)

"There is no limit to what a man can do or where he can go if he does not mind who gets the credit." (Truman)

"If we cannot find contentment in ourselves, it is useless to seek it elsewhere." (La Rochefoucauld)

"If your heart is right, your world will be right. The beginning of all reform must be in yourself. . . . The power released from within yourself will change your outward life." Found at the wall of the U.S. Library of Congress (October 16, 1789)

"To be happy means to be self-sufficient." (Aristotle)

"Unless a person find a mission to devote himself, he cannot find the true happiness." (Found at a Rinzai-ji Temple in Japan)

"A happy life is joy in the truth." (Augustine)

"O wonderful, wonderful, and most wonderful wonderful! And yet again wonderful . . ." (Shakespeare)

"Man is a thinking reed but his great works are done when he is not calculating and thinking. 'Childlikeness' has to be restored with long years of training in the art of 'self-forgetfulness.'" (Daisetz T. Suzuki)

"Truth is too simple for us; we do not like those who unmask our illusion." (Emerson)

"Not knowing how near the truth is, we seek it far away." (Hakuin)

"Everyone wants to understand art. Why not try to understand the songs of a bird?" (Picasso)

"Intelligence comes into being when brain discovers its fallibility." (Krishnamurti)

"Suffering is always the effect of wrong thoughts in some direction. It is an indication that the individual is out of harmony with himself, with the Law of his being." (James Allen)

"Freedom's just another word for nothing left to lose." (Kris Kristofferson)

"A free mind has power to achieve all things." (Eckhart)

"The fruit of the Spirit is love, joy, peace." (Gal. 5:22)

"If you cannot dedicate all your works to the Divine, then do the work without the desire of the fruit." (Bhagavadgita)

"Let the mind flow freely without abiding anywhere." (Diamond Sutra)

"All living being, be peaceful, gentle and happy. Whether animals, plants, big or small, long or short. . . . All living being be happy." (Buddha [Suttanipata 145–147])

"Unless the world as a whole can achieve happiness there is no happiness as an individual. . . . The consciousness as a person will progress from individual to group to society to the universe." (Kenji Miyazawa)

"*It is only with the heart that one can see rightly; what is essential is invisible to the eye.*" (Antoine de Saint-Exupéry)

"*Use the light that is in you to recover your natural clearness of sight.*" (Lao-tzu)

"*There is a treasure in every person.*" (Sufism)

"*. . . the truth is the subject's transformation within himself.*" (Kierkegaard)

"*If you deliberately plan to be less than you are capable of being, I warn you that you will be deeply unhappy for the rest of your life.*" (Abraham Maslow)

"*If you do not have a dream, you might as well be dead.*" (Dixie Rose)

"*I have a dream.*" (Martin Luther King)

"*I think I can, I think I can.*" (*The Little Engine That Could*)

"*May I have the strength to change the things I can, the patience to accept the things I cannot, and the wisdom to know the difference.*" (Saint Francis)

"*To live is the rarest thing in the world. Most people exist, that is all.*" (Oscar Wilde)

"*Be careful . . . not to interfere with the natural goodness of the heart of man.*" (Chuang-Tzu)

"You shall know the truth, and the truth shall make you free." (John 8:32)

"To know all is to forgive all." (French Proverb)

"Do not seek for the steps of the master. Seek what the master aims for." (Japanese Proverb)

"You are your own master, you make your own future." (Buddha [Dhammapada 380])

"Know thyself." (Socrates)

Of these words, which ones resonated with you or reached your heart? Some of us may be satisfied just to get the idea. Others may take time to try to understand the deeper meaning. Few will really live with the idea. Fewer still will share the idea with others to explore what life is all about. Ultimately it is up to us to find the fire within us to explore whatever we find desirable and right on our life's journey.

Appendix D

Characteristics of the Masters

❖

If we think about it, we are all masters of something. Just as we have acquired the skills of eating, speaking, or picking things up, so are we learning something everyday even though we may not be conscious of it. To discover and fully express our potential, the following is an attempt to list the characteristics of the true masters. Ultimately, of course, each of us should develop his or her own unique characteristics.

1. Be sensible to listen to our hearts while distinguishing the key issues from various background noises. The problems we encounter in life do not have to control our lives.

2. Be aware of our own feelings. Do not try to repress them or react prematurely. When we experience negative feelings such as anxiety, anger, depression, greed, or envy, we should analyze our feelings to discover the cause—as if we are the third person watching our own emotion with detachment. The solution will eventually come as an insight and our solid foundation will be regained.

3. Accept reality, fate, uncertainty, and the unknown for what they are. Do not blindly fight against them. Otherwise, we end up being caught up. If there is something that is out of our control, just accept it. We live in

an impermanent world. Understand the laws of nature and find our destiny with whatever resources we have.

4. Visualize the world through the eyes of an innocent child. Instead of seeing trees as always green, and flowers always red, find the subtlety in everything and every event. Instead of being preoccupied with our own thoughts, be flexible to look at things as they are. Pause, observe, and inquire about what is going on every so often to see if our minds are in harmony. Be open to change. Be inquisitive to infinitely varied people, ideas, events, and things surrounding us.

5. Find a mission that fully uses our talent to express our innovative and creative potential. Realize that we are happy when we are one with mission. Be self-directed rather than other-directed. Be original rather than conforming. Be flexible rather than rigid. Live life with a solid foundation connected to our heart.

6. As we find out more about ourselves, consider whether we can identify ourselves with others, and be compassionate to them.

7. Although we are interdependent beings, we should try to seek our own destiny without outside support wherever possible.

8. Be open-minded and flexible about unavoidable difficulties that we all face. Convert negative feelings to constructive energy.

9. Accept unconditionally who we are—whether we perform well, are popular, or have handicaps. Experiences of failure provide feedback to help us realize what does not work. Realize that, ultimately, there is no failure.

10. Experiment and be playful the way a child might explore the mystery in life. Be aware of life in all its manifestations, reflect, plan, and act to move on.

11. If we do not explore, learn, appreciate and strive, why are we here? This process itself is self-actualizing.

In this book, we have discussed the need for the heart and brain to be connected to channel our energy and express our talent as it is meant to be. The search for answers will continue in our everyday life while proof of our efforts needs to be shown—and will be shown even if nobody asks for it. Individuals may be characterized as "heart-heavy" or "brain-heavy." Since each of our lives is different, our specific journeys will vary. On occasion, we may feel lost or vulnerable and unable to find our way. Yet to live our lives, we must go through these rough patches. If someone asks "Why?" we shall say "Why not?"

Acknowledgments

✦

In one fall season, I had seminars in three cities in Spain. I presented an overall view of the mini-company, followed by implementation cases by people who had practiced the idea. Even though we did not communicate in advance, the people from UBISA, a Bekaert Group company, which won the European Quality Prize, also covered the topic of brain and heart. They emphasized that it is the heart that is the core of the mini-company and made their presentation centered on that theme. Listening to their presentation, I was quite moved that we identified with something that is very essential in running the mini-company.

We all have such connecting moments. And I have had many of them in the course of my career. In such moments, we may not directly share feelings verbally, but there is that sparkling light in the eyes and sense of spirit in the air that is beyond expression. Only quietude with full awareness seems most fit to such moments. Also, reflecting back on the people who expressed negative feeling about my seminars or the ideas of the mini-company, I thank them, because without them I would not have faced the challenge and brought even more energy, courage, and will to explore what can be made possible. Even if I am only imagining this whole process and my whole life experience is a dream, is it not still good if each of us can believe in such a dream, wishing to achieve a state of grace that will spread compassion and forbearance throughout the world?

I have referred to literally hundreds of books and many years of personal experiences as a base of this book. As I cannot single out even twenty or fifty of them, I have decided not to mention any specifically. What I believe is that even a single line in a book or a short encounter with a person has influenced me to a degree that I cannot measure. I hope this book will be seen as a collection of wisdom derived from all of these encounters.

I thank all of you and all events that took place in the past. I appreciate that collectively this book expresses the voice and experiences of all those with whom I have been affiliated. I recognize limitations in myself, but I still hope your voices are passed on through this book. After all, we are ultimately a representation of the heart expressed in various forms. So, it may be most appropriate that I thank the heart for making this endeavor possible.

As seeds of flowers will travel even to a faraway land and start new roots there, I believe the best acknowledgment that I can think of would be the transmission of the messages expressed in our various life activities. In business or any other life activities, expressions may take place in whatever form by whomever, whenever, wherever, or however. So, thank you all and I wish the best on your journey!

For those who wish to share thoughts or experiences related to the mini-company on the Internet, please visit Yahoo! Club Mini-company at http://clubs.yahoo.com/clubs/minicompany

My home page is at http://www.geocities.com/suzakico/index.html

Index

About the Author

❖

Starting his career at Toshiba as an engineer in Japan, Kiyoshi Suzaki earned his MBA from Stanford, and worked at the Boston Consulting Group on corporate strategy. As the president of Suzaki & Company, he traveled to some thirty countries to conduct seminars, and consulted to more than a hundred companies. In this book Suzaki has condensed what he considers the core management principles for everyone to practice. He is also the author of *The New Manufacturing Challenge* (The Free Press) and *The New Shop Floor Management* (The Free Press).